Design Firms
OPEN
FOR BUSINESS

STEVEN HELLER AND LITA TALARICO

ALLWORTH PRESS
NEW YORK

DESIGN

OP

FOR BU

STEVEN HELLEP

FIRMS

EN

SINESS

AND LITA TALARICO

FOR LOUISE + NICK — S.H.
FOR JULIAN — L.T.

Allworth Press books may be purchased in bulk at special discounts for
sales promotion, corporate gifts, fund-raising, or educational purposes.
Special editions can also be created to specifications. For details, contact the
Special Sales Department, Allworth Press, 307 West 36th Street, 11th Floor,
New York, NY 10018 or info@skyhorsepublishing.com.
15 14 13 12 11   5 4 3 2 1

Published by Allworth Press, an imprint of Skyhorse Publishing, Inc.
307 West 36th Street, 11th Floor, New York, NY 10018. Allworth Press® is a
registered trademark of Skyhorse Publishing, Inc.®, a Delaware corporation.

www.allworth.com

Cover and interior design by RED / Rogers Eckersley Design

Library of Congress Cataloging-in-Publication Data is available on file.
ISBN: 978-1-58115-930-1

Printed in China

ACKNOWLEDGMENTS

This book (and so many others) would not be possible if not for the continued support and enthusiasm of Tad Crawford, who has led Allworth Press for many fruitful years. We thank him for everything he's done for graphic design and design writing. We are also grateful to Delia Casa, assistant editor at Skyhorse Publishing, for her keen attention to this project.

Of course, the stars of this book are the designers who are featured—and even some of those who are not. To you we are most grateful.

And for their continued support, thanks to David Rhodes, president, and Anthony Rhodes, executive vice president of the School of Visual Arts, New York.

Finally, much appreciation to Esther Ro-Schofield and Ron Callahan at the SVA MFA Design / Designer as Author + Entrepreneur program for their good humor, hard work, and attention to details.

– STEVEN HELLER & LITA TALARICO

CONT

SECTION ONE: SMALL FIRMS
1-8 EMPLOYEES

ENTS

SECTION TWO: MEDIUM FIRMS
9-14 EMPLOYEES

SECTION THREE: LARGE FIRMS
15+ EMPLOYEES

OPEN FOR BUSINESS

OPENING A DESIGN OFFICE IS AN ACT OF PROFESSIONAL MATURITY, LIKE GETTING A FIRST CAR, A FIRST APARTMENT, AND EVEN A FIRST COUCH.

Signing the lease, hanging a sign on the door, selecting the perfect furniture, and placing inspiring art on the walls are coming-of-age rituals that never get tiresome. For some designers the ritual is therefore repeated many times, while others spend many contented years in their long-term rentals. Indeed the expense of renting space often leads to another maturity-affirming act—buying real estate. Property ownership increases the ritualistic intensity and underscores pride-of-place emotions.

A designer's workplace is a self-defining environment, a showcase of sense and sensibility, a window to the mind of the professional, and maybe the heart, too. What a designer chooses to display in the space reveals how important the details (as Mies van der Rohe famously noted in his statement about God being in them) really are. Whether or not comfort is a factor is also telltale. A workplace without comfy amenities for guests says one thing, whereas a space with generous reception and meeting areas says another. The office is such a charged environment that some designers establish strict rules to govern behavior. Massimo Vignelli's storied dictum that there must be no personal ephemera pinned to an individual's workspace implied two things: That the designers did not command their own workstations (in other words, they were interchangeable); and that personal clutter must not mar the overall design aesthetic. Conversely, certain designers encourage (or are at least laissez-faire) about decorative diversity and workplace clutter, as they are evidence of a vigorous creative environment.

Design spaces, as reflective of creative people in general, are rarely neutral. Rather they are expressions of something important—intimacy or power, or both—that is being communicated to clients, staff, visitors, or simply the messenger. As in handwriting analysis, it is worthwhile to unpack a designer's intentions, but in this book we will forego inquiry into the pseudo-psychological under-pinnings of office design. Instead we introduce various designers who are *Open for Business* in spaces that are either modest or lavish, according to their preference. This is not, however, a book about workspaces alone. It is rather a study of the people who inhabit those spaces, and whose creative practices are engaged with the places where they conceive ideas and collaborate with others.

The principals of each studio featured herein answered a common volley of questions. Some are delightfully loquacious; others are self-consciously succinct. Nonetheless, each tells the story of why their studio was formed, why they chose its name, and where it is housed. Questions about design philosophy and aesthetics are balanced with the nitty-gritty of their businesses (staffing, client types, expansion, etc.). Individually, they offer insight into why studios are formed. Collectively, they may provide models for those who are considering the plunge.

We have chosen to represent a broad range of designers in terms of geography, age, and experience, operating small (one to eight), medium (nine to fourteen), and large (fifteen-plus) firms, and even a few without any employees. Independent designers, we found, are increasingly likely to start with small full-time staffs, relying on freelance help when necessary. They are, surprisingly, investing their capital into their studios. Building a sturdy yet scalable infrastructure is, in today's economy, more important than creating a staff, which invariably will ebb and flow as clients come and go. Designers are more comfortable when they are not carrying financial burdens, which obviously means not having to accept commissions that portend difficulty or take on difficult clients simply to pay the salaries of their staffs.

When opening a design firm, understanding that bigger is not better is vital to the firm's success, as is accepting fiscal and creative responsibility. It is also an act of professional maturity. The designers who comprise *Design Firms Open for Business*, regardless of style, manner, and preference, have this in common.

– STEVEN HELLER AND LITA TALARICO

ADAMS MORIOKA

ANDE + PARTNERS

ANZELEVICH

BASE ART CO.

CIRCLE

DESIGN IS PLAY

DESIGN CENTER LTD.

FELIX SOCKWELL, INC

DONDINA ASSOCIATI

DESIGN: L'ORANGE

IGARASHI STUDIO

MELCHIOR IMBODEN

JAMES VICTORE INC.

EL JEFE DESIGN

J.J. SEDELMAIER PRODUCTIONS, INC

JOEL KATZ DESIGN ASSOCIATES

KARLSSONWILKER INC

KEITH GODARD

KIND COMPANY

LANDERS MILLER DESIGN

LSDSPACE/UN MUNDO FELIZ

MASONBARONET

MGMT. DESIGN

PIETRO CORRAINI

PLURAL

RED

SAGMEISTER INC.

SAWDUST

344 DESIGN, LLC

STUDIO LAUCKE SIEBEIN

TAREK ATRISSI DESIGN

THESUMOF

VERTIGO DESIGN

SECTION ONE:

SMALL FIRMS

1-8 EMPLOYEES

ADAMS MORIOKA

WHAT PROMPTED YOU TO START A STUDIO?

In the early 1990s, the design world was focused on a dystopian, chaotic, degenerated, and oblique approach. We wanted to create work that was clear, simple, optimistic, and accessible. Starting a firm was the only way to achieve this.

HOW DID YOU DETERMINE WHERE YOUR STUDIO WOULD BE LOCATED?

At first, we thought we could work out of my house. This became an episode of *Please Don't Eat the Daisies*: the phone ringing, dog barking, messengers at the door, and soup boiling over. The architect Barton Myers offered us space in his office in Beverly Hills. He was generous and suggested that we trade services for rent. We moved to a larger space a couple of years later. We are still in Beverly Hills, specifically in the Larry Flynt building. The studio is centrally located between Downtown and the West Side of Los Angeles. It is easy for clients to access. It has remarkable views and great security (à la Larry Flynt). Contrary to popular opinion, there are no naked women, as the Hustler filming happens elsewhere (probably in the Valley).

PRINCIPALS
SEAN ADAMS
NOREEN MORIOKA

FOUNDED
1990

LOCATION
BEVERLY HILLS, CA

EMPLOYEES
8

THIS SPREAD: Mexico Restaurant **CLIENT:** Larry Nicola **CREATIVE DIRECTOR:** Sean Adams
DESIGNERS: Sean Adams, Monica Schlaug, Chris Taillion

DESCRIBE YOUR AESTHETIC, STYLISTIC (EVEN PHILOSOPHIC) APPROACH TO DESIGN.

At heart, we follow the principles of clarity, purity, and resonance (design "CPR"). "Clarity" refers to the accessibility of the message. The communication should be understandable to a wide audience, not just five people attending an avant-garde performance festival. Creating work that is purposely oblique and difficult to access is an elitist and exclusionary act. "Purity" refers to form. If something isn't needed, it isn't there. This doesn't translate as minimalism. A solution may require a dense form, but there is nothing purely decorative or arbitrary. "Resonance" is about emotional connection. Without this, the work could easily become cold and distant. The emotional connection can happen in multiple ways. Seduction, levity, and humor, however, have been consistent themes over the last eighteen years.

WHAT IS THE REASON FOR THE NAME OF YOUR STUDIO?

It's our own names. Choosing a name that sounds like a band didn't make any sense since we don't play instruments, we're not groovy, we don't live in Brooklyn, and we don't wear jaunty hats.

HOW MANY EMPLOYEES (FULL-TIME AND FREELANCE)?

Eight.

HOW MANY PRINCIPALS AND EMPLOYEES ARE DESIGNERS?

Five.

OTHERS?

Administrative, business, and account management.

DO YOU HAVE A STRATEGIST OR ACCOUNT PERSON ON STAFF?

Yes; Noreen handles client relations (whatever that entails) and works directly with most clients. After the initial strategy and direction are established, the day-to-day communication transfers. At this point one of the designers or I manage the process. It may be antiquated, but I believe designers do better work when they are responsible for a project and speak directly to a client.

DESCRIBE YOUR CLIENTELE.

We're fortunate to have a national client base, with a few international ones. The work is primarily identity and systems, signage, and web. In entertainment: the Academy of Motion Picture Arts and Sciences, Disney, Wasserman, Sundance; medical institutions: Cedars-Sinai; finance: the Glowacki Group; education: USC, UCLA, Curtis Institute of Music, Santa Monica College; nonprofits: the Broad Foundation, the Library Foundation, the Natural History Museum; architecture: Richard Meier and Partners, Barton Myers Architects, Frank Gehry Partners, Fred Fisher and Partners.

ARE YOU ATTEMPTING TO BROADEN YOUR CLIENT BASE?

At one point we thought it would be fun to work with more clients in Japan. But now we're old, and spending eighteen hours in a plane is no fun.

DO YOU SPECIALIZE? OR GENERALIZE?

We generalize. Our attention span is short and we would be bored doing only one activity.

ARE YOU PRIMARILY PRINT OR VIRTUAL, OR BOTH?

Both; most projects are larger identity and programmatic systems that require print, online, environmental, and social media applications.

HOW MUCH FREEDOM TO YOU ALLOW INDIVIDUAL DESIGNERS?

I have been told that I have a Ronald Reagan management style. This may refer to my being out of touch, but I hope it is about a hands-off approach. The designers have an innate sensibility that is similar to Noreen's and mine. They each bring something unique to the table but don't ride off the rails. Over the years we have had designers who rebelled against the firm's approach and attempted to make solutions that had meaningless squiggles, or—worst of all—collage. They required too much direction and didn't last.

HOW WOULD YOU DEFINE COLLABORATION AS PRACTICED IN YOUR STUDIO?

AdamsMorioka isn't the kind of studio that has group crits. I'm not interested in interrupting everyone's day to sit in a conference room and wax on about each solution. Each designer takes a lead on a project. I may give some initial direction and check in, and then he or she takes responsibility for the project. Collaboration with us typically means standing next to someone who says, "Does this look dumb?"

COULD YOUR STUDIO GET ALONG WITHOUT YOU FOR ANY PERIOD OF TIME?

They probably operate better. This was put to the test during my AIGA presidency. I was out of the office traveling a couple of days or more a week. Everything worked well, although there was the extra burden of missing one designer from the workload. And they probably mixed margaritas all day.

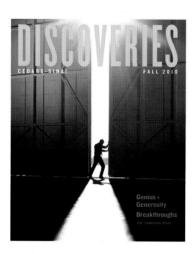

Cedars-Sinai *Discoveries* magazine **CLIENT:** Cedars-Sinai **EDITOR:** Laura Grunberger **CREATIVE DIRECTOR:** Sean Adams **DESIGNERS:** Sean Adams, Monica Schlaug, Nathan Stock

DO YOU HAVE A LONG-TERM PLAN FOR SUSTAINABILITY OR GROWTH?

We don't want to grow in manpower, but I'm perfectly fine with profit growth. At times when we have had a larger studio, we've been at our lowest creatively. We also saw decreased profit and joy of work. We maintain a reasonable size in order to have the luxury of turning down work and focusing on clients and projects we value. This wouldn't work if each person here weren't extraordinarily efficient, talented, and smart.

WHAT IS THE MOST CHALLENGING PART OF HAVING A STUDIO?

Having a studio. When people ask me if they should start their own design business, I typically ask them if they are entrepreneurial. If you are, then yes, start your own business. If you aren't, you shouldn't. Either option is valid. The most challenging part of owning a design studio is the relentless nature inherent in any small business. Finding new work, producing, and meeting revenue goals is a never-ending job.

DESCRIBE THE MOST SATISFYING PROJECT(S) OF THE PAST YEAR.

It's been a challenging year. I've found that most of our clients are fearful of losing their jobs, whether they're CEOs or marketing directors. Consequently, every decision is heavily weighed, and fewer clients are willing to take bolder steps. Some projects, however, have been enormously enjoyable. I've been working on Mohawk Paper's Via line for several years. Mohawk is a dream client: smart, experienced, clear, and good people. I suggested a focus on American idioms and ideas as a backdrop to exemplify specific processes for ink on paper. Most of the imagery came from the Library of Congress Prints and Photographs collection. And I was able to weave in my own family connections with an image of Samuel Clemens, the Fry and Jefferson map of Virginia, and Mount Vernon. The end product is one of my favorite pieces, and I loved the process.

Mohawk Via Printing and Paper **CLIENT:** Mohawk Fine Papers **CREATIVE DIRECTOR:** Sean Adams
DESIGNER: Sean Adams

ANDE + PARTNERS

WHAT IS THE REASON FOR THE NAME OF YOUR STUDIO?

I'm able to do my most satisfying work when the clients are partners in the process. Listening to them, working closely, and understanding what their real needs are. Usually when everyone is deeply involved, the final result ends up being visually smart, the message is clear, and the client's bottom line improves.

HOW LONG HAVE YOU HAD A STUDIO?

Since 1996, in some form or other.

HOW MANY EMPLOYEES (FULL-TIME AND FREELANCE)?

We are a small company, under five. If it's a film project or a large re-brand we can freelance up to nine. I have trouble managing more than that.

HOW MANY PRINCIPALS AND EMPLOYEES ARE DESIGNERS?

Everyone on my team has a strong type and design background.

OTHERS?

I always try to involve a non-designer, someone who speaks design fluently, but can be an objective sounding board.

DO YOU HAVE A STRATEGIST OR ACCOUNT PERSON ON STAFF?

I do the strategy and project management.

DESCRIBE YOUR CLIENTELE.

Our clients range from Fortune 500 companies to local entrepreneurs.

ARE YOU ATTEMPTING TO BROADEN YOUR CLIENT BASE?

Always. When you work on the same type of projects over and over, you get burned out.

DO YOU SPECIALIZE? OR GENERALIZE?

We specialize in branding and identity development, but that can apply to a very general audience. Our process has been successful for packaging, websites, films, campaigns, and most things in between.

ARE YOU PRIMARILY PRINT OR VIRTUAL, OR BOTH?

Both.

WHAT PROMPTED YOU TO START A STUDIO?

I sold an idea and needed something to put on the invoice. I was very naive at the time and had no idea what I was getting into.

HOW DID YOU DETERMINE WHERE YOUR STUDIO WOULD BE LOCATED?

Close to home, family, and good places to eat.

DESCRIBE YOUR AESTHETIC, STYLISTIC (EVEN PHILOSOPHIC) APPROACH TO DESIGN.

I have trouble with questions like this. I'm not sure if we have a "house style." I guess one common thread is strong typography; I think that is important because it's what your voice looks like. We are very witty. Smart, but not condescending. A lot of our work is also accessible. A lot of people from diverse backgrounds get it.

PRINCIPAL
ANDE LA MONICA

FOUNDED
2004

LOCATION
HOBOKEN, NJ

EMPLOYEES
**4 FULL-TIME
AND FREELANCE**

HOW MUCH FREEDOM DO YOU ALLOW INDIVIDUAL DESIGNERS?

I give my team a lot of freedom in the beginning. In order for them to be good at what we do, there needs to be a bit of "play" involved. I rein them in as the project goes forward.

HOW WOULD YOU DEFINE COLLABORATION AS PRACTICED IN YOUR STUDIO?

We all work on everything together. It's hard to design in a vacuum.

COULD YOUR STUDIO GET ALONG WITHOUT YOU FOR ANY PERIOD OF TIME?

I look forward to that day.

DO YOU HAVE A LONG-TERM PLAN FOR SUSTAINABILITY OR GROWTH?

I never had a formal business plan, but that may bite me in the ass one day. My long-term plan for sustainability and growth revolves around a strong fear of failure. We work hard and put the time in, we take on clients that we like, I nurture my team, we return phone calls promptly, and we aspire to do relevant work.

WHAT IS THE MOST CHALLENGING PART OF HAVING A STUDIO?

The work/life balance.

DESCRIBE THE MOST SATISFYING PROJECT(S) OF THE PAST YEAR.

We were asked by Bloomberg LP, a global financial and media company, to help develop a wellness campaign for their employees. The project was about helping their employees be more informed and make better health decisions. The project took over our office for quite some time. About a year later, I was standing in their lobby and on large screens they were profiling success stories from the campaign: one man lost fifty pounds, another woman quit smoking, one after another. It was very inspiring to work with Bloomberg and develop something that had an immediate effect on people to make their lives better.

We were also asked to re-brand a sports nutrition company. Identity, packaging, website, marketing materials… everything. The marketplace for sports nutrition is overrun with bad design. Products look the same, companies copy each other's style, and they are not transparent about what goes in the product or the purity of the ingredients. Our client actually has a great product and they pride themselves on making it from the highest quality ingredients. They just didn't know how to effectively reach their audience. It was satisfying to see how much the success of the company was directly related to the effectiveness of the design. Since the re-brand, their sales have increased greatly, they have a stronger consumer awareness, the company is growing, and we were able to give a visual breath of fresh air to the marketplace.

(TOP) Match 10 learning system **(BOTTOM)** The package design component of the rebrand for Beast Sports Nutrition.

ANZELEVICH

WHAT PROMPTED YOU TO START A STUDIO?

I returned to Israel with the desire to try and maintain the drive and interest I felt in New York, which led me to open my own studio, where I could apply my own philosophy and ideas.

HOW DID YOU DETERMINE WHERE YOUR STUDIO WOULD BE LOCATED?

The studio is located in the "old north" of Tel Aviv near the beach, close to where I lived when I founded it. It is a quiet and pastoral area just five minutes from the city center.

DESCRIBE YOUR AESTHETIC, STYLISTIC (EVEN PHILOSOPHIC) APPROACH TO DESIGN.

"Thought has to pass through the heart to be made active and meaningful." –Henry Miller

We bring to our day-to-day work various influences and inspirations that are an integral part of the studio: inspirations from daily life, nature, ready-made materials, a visit to the flea market, a trip to New York, museums, or just browsing a magazine. Sources of inspiration are everywhere around us all the time; we just take them and use them as raw material for a new creation that bears our mark.

WHAT IS THE REASON FOR THE NAME OF YOUR STUDIO?

The studio is named after the owner.

HOW LONG HAVE YOU HAD A STUDIO?

The studio opened in 2003, shortly after I returned to Israel from New York, where I studied at SVA and worked at Kiehl's studio in Manhattan.

HOW MANY EMPLOYEES (FULL-TIME AND FREELANCE)?

We have three designers at the studio working full-time together with a marketing director.

OTHERS?

We work in partnership with strategists, copywriters, illustrators, and programmers as needed, according to the nature of the project.

DO YOU HAVE A STRATEGIST OR ACCOUNT PERSON ON STAFF?

No, we bring together the perfect team for each project according to its needs.

DESCRIBE YOUR CLIENTELE.

We work with a wide range of clients from various industries, such as culture and art, lifestyle, real estate, food, technology, government offices, NGOs, and private clients.

ARE YOU ATTEMPTING TO BROADEN YOUR CLIENT BASE?

The studio's ambition is to work with a wide range of clients, so we work daily on expanding our client base.

DO YOU SPECIALIZE? OR GENERALIZE?

Dealing with a wide variety of clients and projects provides us with challenges that help keep the studio—and, ultimately, our work process—interesting.

PRINCIPAL
YIFAT ANZELEVICH

FOUNDED
2003

LOCATION
TEL AVIV, ISRAEL

EMPLOYEES
3 FULL-TIME

The studio—"where the magic happens." **PHOTOS:** Yanai Yehiel

ARE YOU PRIMARILY PRINT OR VIRTUAL, OR BOTH?

My love and passion lie in the world of print, but of course digital media are an integral part of any project.

HOW MUCH FREEDOM DO YOU ALLOW INDIVIDUAL DESIGNERS?

I believe in giving the designers at the studio the freedom to create. All three of us contribute to each project, no matter who leads it. I think that by collaborating this way, we bring uniqueness to the project, and this creates a new and refreshing result every time.

COULD YOUR STUDIO GET ALONG WITHOUT YOU FOR ANY PERIOD OF TIME?

Our team can function at all times, even if I am not at the studio.

DO YOU HAVE A LONG-TERM PLAN FOR SUSTAINABILITY OR GROWTH?

Graphic design is an integral part of my life, and if we stay a small studio, I can still be involved in all our projects.

WHAT IS THE MOST CHALLENGING PART OF HAVING A STUDIO?

Finding a balance between managing the day-to-day work at the studio and being a graphic designer.

DESCRIBE THE MOST SATISFYING PROJECT(S) OF THE PAST YEAR.

In the past year we started to design and produce unique products that combine magnets and paper products. The special experience of designing a product without a client, a product that expresses our creativity and passion, opened a new world for us.

(TOP) *Teza* ABOUT: Design and image editing of the Tel Aviv University student magazine PHOTO: Yanai Yehiel (BOTTOM) A set of greeting cards with magnets printed on natural fabric PHOTO: Yanai Yehiel

Stage Center **ABOUT:** Informative and identity site for the Stage Center, which holds diverse training workshops in the performing arts **PHOTO:** Yanai Yehiel

BASE
ART CO.

WHAT IS THE REASON FOR THE NAME OF YOUR STUDIO?

I wish I had a great story here… but sixteen years ago, I thought "Base" was just a cool name (I actually had the name a few years before making it official). A few years later, a large ad agency in town renamed themselves similarly, and there was a bit too much confusion with the two of our names. Consequently, I added "Art Co." to give us some distinction.

HOW LONG HAVE YOU HAD A STUDIO?

The studio was born August 1997.

HOW MANY EMPLOYEES (FULL-TIME AND FREELANCE)?

Three full-time.

HOW MANY PRINCIPALS AND EMPLOYEES ARE DESIGNERS?

All are designers.

DO YOU HAVE A STRATEGIST OR ACCOUNT PERSON ON STAFF?

No. We have a great network of talented collaborators—for our strategy, copywriting, information architecture, and development needs. We love this approach, as we're able to bring the best of class to each project, ramping up and down as needed.

PRINCIPAL
TERRY ROHRBACH

FOUNDED
1997

LOCATION
COLUMBUS, OHIO

EMPLOYEES
3 FULL-TIME

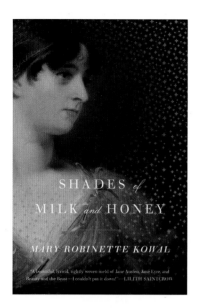

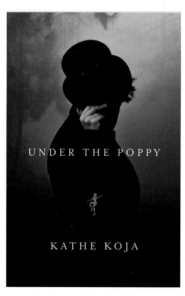

DESCRIBE YOUR CLIENTELE.

Our client list is a national assortment of nonprofits, corporate giants, publishing houses, and startups. We greatly value our opportunities, and have been very successful in forging long-term client relationships that are built on trust. Most of our client relationships are connected directly to the business owner or primary stakeholders. We like that, as it cuts communication gaps, and helps us gain truer insights into the communication problem or need.

ARE YOU ATTEMPTING TO BROADEN YOUR CLIENT BASE?

Yes. Although we are "generalists," there are certain niches we see opportunities in, including education and nonprofit branding/interactive. Additionally, we are trying to develop retainer relationships.

DO YOU SPECIALIZE? OR GENERALIZE?

We specialize in creativity. So that enables us to work on projects ranging from print collateral and event exhibit design to branding and interactive.

ARE YOU PRIMARILY PRINT OR VIRTUAL, OR BOTH?

Currently we have a mix of 60 percent print/branding and 40 percent digital. Our roots are definitely in print design, but we have successfully crossed the bridge to be just as proficient in digital. I predict in a few years our mix may flip to 60 percent digital… We're finding that the exciting and constantly evolving world of digital design offers a lot of opportunities for growth, which is alluring.

WHAT PROMPTED YOU TO START A STUDIO?

I had the great pleasure of working with great people (and at great places) early in my career. But it was always my intention to start my own studio. My passion is design, but I also enjoy the business side. I really coveted the ability to be a generalist, work directly with my clients, and do the work that makes me most happy.

HOW DID YOU DETERMINE WHERE YOUR STUDIO WOULD BE LOCATED?

I'm originally from the East Coast (Philadelphia) but came to Columbus, Ohio to be a Buckeye at the Ohio State University. Columbus has proven to be a great spot for Base Art Co.; its central location allows us to work seamlessly with outfits in New York, Texas, and Atlanta. (Of course, the advent of email and the Internet has made it possible for everyone to work remotely with ease…) Columbus also boasts great industry and a strong client base, which has thankfully allowed my business to thrive. Within Columbus, I specifically chose to work in the bustling arts district of the Short North, home to multitudes of galleries, boutiques, and restaurants. There's always something going on right outside of our windows!

DESCRIBE YOUR AESTHETIC, STYLISTIC (EVEN PHILOSOPHIC) APPROACH TO DESIGN.

We strive to create simplistic beauty. We try to avoid getting locked into a specific design style or relying on a "company look," and instead focus on the problem and how it can best be solved visually.

Tegan and Sara Concert Poster **ABOUT:** A limited edition silkscreen poster promoting Tegan and Sara's Columbus, Ohio concert. The angel spinning a skull web plays on the duality of twins and the album name, "Sainthood." **CLIENT:** PromoWest Productions **DESIGN:** Drue Dixon, Terry Rohrbach

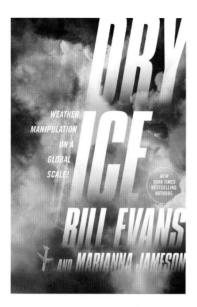

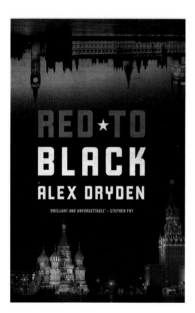

(TOP) *Dry Ice* book cover **CLIENT:** Tor Books
CREATIVE DIRECTOR: Irene Gallo
(BOTTOM) *Red to Black* book cover **CLIENT:** Harp-
erCollins **CREATIVE DIRECTOR:** Allison Saltzman
DESIGNER: Terry Rohrbach **PHOTOGRAPHY:** Jeremy
Walker and Dean Conger/Getty Images

HOW MUCH FREEDOM DO YOU ALLOW INDIVIDUAL DESIGNERS?

Everybody is encouraged to develop ideas and concepts, and collectively we come to the most appropriate response to the design challenge.

HOW WOULD YOU DEFINE COLLABORATION AS PRACTICED IN YOUR STUDIO?

We have an open studio floor plan with all the workstations centered in the room. This allows us to easily share ideas and offer each other immediate feedback on individual projects. That said, we also strive to bring our clients and partners in as collaborators, and we all construc-tively work toward the best solutions.

COULD YOUR STUDIO GET ALONG WITHOUT YOU FOR ANY PERIOD OF TIME?

I have complete trust in the capabili-ties of our team to function without me. However, because of the work-load and expectations of our clients, it's difficult.

DO YOU HAVE A LONG-TERM PLAN FOR SUSTAINABILITY OR GROWTH?

After fourteen years with three full-time employees (including me), it's become obvious my goal is not growth in terms of staff. I'm com-mitted to working with people who share my passion for great design and business success. And quite frankly, those perfect matches are hard to find. Plans for sustainability include creating and maintaining re-tainer and/or multifaceted accounts with many touchpoints. Of course, we're also always trying to stay current and take full advantage of new opportunities in the flourishing digital space.

WHAT IS THE MOST CHALLENGING PART OF HAVING A STUDIO?

As a small studio, we are all required to wear many hats and perform at a high level of efficiency and creativity. I'm lucky to have found two great de-signers who share my same values and work ethic.

DESCRIBE THE MOST SATISFYING PROJECT(S) OF THE PAST YEAR.

We serve as brand partner for Pelotonia, a grassroots cycling event where 100 percent of all funds raised directly support cancer research conducted at the Comprehensive Cancer Center and James Cancer Hospital/Solove Research Institute at the Ohio State University. Each year I personally participate by riding 102 miles. Lead by a visionary CEO, the organization pushes us to evolve and refresh the look each year. And touchpoints extend across the realms of web and advertising to environ-mental design and video direction.

Pelotonia **ABOUT:** Pelotonia is an annual cycling event that donates 100 percent of proceeds to innovative and life-saving cancer research at the James, the premier cancer hospital and research institute at the Ohio State University. **CLIENT:** Pelotonia **CREATIVE DIRECTOR:** Terry Rohrbach **DESIGNERS:** Terry Rohrbach, Drue Dixon, Meredith Reuter

PRINCIPAL
ROBERT L. PETERS

FOUNDED
1976

LOCATION
WINNIPEG, CANADA

EMPLOYEES
3 FULL-TIME
1 PART-TIME
SOME FREELANCE

CIRCLE

WHAT IS THE REASON FOR THE NAME OF YOUR STUDIO?
A holistic worldview that is inclusive and nonhierarchical. A circle is also a universal form/archetype representing wholeness, completion, and autonomy.

HOW LONG HAVE YOU HAD A STUDIO?
Since April 1, 1976 (35+ years).

HOW MANY EMPLOYEES (FULL-TIME AND FREELANCE)?
Three full-time, one part-time, plus contracted freelancers.

HOW MANY PRINCIPALS AND EMPLOYEES ARE DESIGNERS?
Three of us are designers. The other is our "coordinator," who takes care of most internal non-design functions as well as client-facing administrative activities.

DESCRIBE YOUR CLIENTELE.
We have a diverse mix of clients, ranging from local small- and medium-sized businesses to several national corporations, and some international customers. Due to the fact that we are not located in a "head office" city, in concert with an "ethical bar" that is set quite high, we tend not to work with multinational corporations. (We do not take on clients or projects unless everyone in our firm agrees that this will make the world a better place and/or that we could in good conscience use their products or services, and everyone who works at Circle has veto power. This means that we would never take on a client involved in, for example, factory farming or GMOs, nonsustainable energy production, or manufacturing of useless plastic products.)

DO YOU SPECIALIZE? OR GENERALIZE?
We are without a doubt generalists, and we believe in the power of lateral thinking. Our ability to "think sideways" is often seen as a real asset by the clients we work with who are at the top of their (specialist) game, but who find themselves in vertical knowledge silos. Being generalists allows us to bring more holistic thinking to our role as strategic consultants and virtual dreamers as well, thanks to a "broader field of vision."

ARE YOU PRIMARILY PRINT OR VIRTUAL, OR BOTH?
We work in print as well as in digital/dynamic media…. Approximately half of what we currently do manifests itself in online branding, communication, and information assets. Most of our work is B2B; very little of what we do ends up being seen directly by consumers (with the exception of the highly visible stamps that we design for Canada Post and other social, cultural, or public information campaigns).

HOW DID YOU DETERMINE WHERE YOUR STUDIO WOULD BE LOCATED?

The need to obtain a job after graduating from college as a graphic designer (in Winnipeg, in Manitoba, where I had moved when I married a Canadian girl who I had originally met in England), as well as the observation that there were many needs for better visual communication design. I had grown up in Europe, and western Canada seemed like somewhat of a design frontier, holding much potential for making a positive impact.

DESCRIBE YOUR AESTHETIC, STYLISTIC (EVEN PHILOSOPHIC) APPROACH TO DESIGN.

Circle Design Incorporated is a firm of graphic designers and visual communicators. Since our formation in 1976 we have helped hundreds of clients conceive winning strategies, implement distinctive corporate identities and brands, and transform information into powerful communication and targeted marketing materials that bring outstanding results.

We are image engineers, information architects, communication designers (and sometimes surrogate dreamers). We solve problems and create opportunities. Although our clients vary dramatically in size and purpose, they share with us a high regard for strategic thinking and a passion for excellence.

We see design as a purposeful, goal-oriented activity that delivers positive results. Good design initiates, simplifies, clarifies, informs, and adds value. At Circle, we help clients stand out from the crowd and cut through the clutter.

We have a vision of a world that is peaceful, balanced, and equitable for all… a colorful world in which diversity is celebrated and differences

Photos
Ginette Reno : Carl Lessard Photographe
Bruce Cockburn : Kevin Kelly
Kate & Anna McGarrigle : Just Loomis
Robbie Robertson : David Jordan Williams
Crowd / Foule : Kativ / iStockphoto

Lowe-Martin
Design : CIRCLE

CANADIAN RECORDING ARTISTS

ARTISTES CANADIENS DE LA CHANSON

(ABOVE) Commemorative postage
stamps featuring Canadian record-
ing artists **CLIENT:** Canada Post **(OPPO-
SITE)** Corporate design for Canada's
oldest retailer **CLIENT:** The Northwest
Company

HAVE A MISSION • PLAN AHEAD
QUESTION EVERYTHING • LISTEN
COLLABORATE • ASSUME NOTHING
STUDY THE PAST • KEEP IT SIMPLE
COMMUNICATE • DRAW A DIAGRAM
NEVER SELL OUT • PUSH HARDER
SAY WHAT YOU MEAN • BE OPEN
ROLL UP YOUR SLEEVES • DREAM
WELCOME CHANGE • ADD VALUE
AIM HIGHER • FOSTER INTUITION
DO MORE WITH LESS • LAUGH
INNOVATE • THINK SIDEWAYS
FOCUS • MEAN WHAT YOU SAY
TAKE IT TO THE EDGE • RELAX

CIRCLE

are embraced… a world in which stimulated human beings live creative, thoughtful lives in harmony with nature… a world in which faith rises above fear, and in which abundance alleviates suffering.

We think of design as the "application of intent." Our mission is to design—to use our collective intellect, talents, and abilities in the service of clients, projects, and initiatives that make a positive difference in shaping the world we envision.

Our clients expect remarkable results. They come to us because we understand the context of an individual problem, because we bring a new perspective to their business challenges, and because we provide them with a competitive advantage. They expect innovative thinking, and they expect us to add value.

To meet these expectations, we work in a methodical, disciplined manner. Our tacticians and practitioners assess needs, harness the creative process, and then utilize the necessary skills, tools, and resources to implement effective design solutions.

HOW MUCH FREEDOM DO YOU ALLOW INDIVIDUAL DESIGNERS?

I'd like to think that designers have much creative freedom, provided that necessary precedents (e.g., existing brand vocabulary, etc.) are taken into consideration. We always define and present design criteria in advance of ideation and creative design exploration; we then return to these criteria when selecting the most appropriate and effective direction to refine and present to the client.

HOW WOULD YOU DEFINE COLLABORATION AS PRACTICED IN YOUR STUDIO?

Projects are handled in a variety of ways, depending on the specific parameters of the engagement and the challenge to be fulfilled. Sometimes the whole creative team jumps in together at the outset, and we ideate and then solve the problem together as a group. Other times it's more like a relay race, with one individual "handing off" to another upon completion of a distinct phase. Regardless, we almost always look to each other to provide critiques and evaluate a proposed solution's appropriateness with regard to the design problem.

COULD YOUR STUDIO GET ALONG WITHOUT YOU FOR ANY PERIOD OF TIME?

Indeed, it could, and has. Between 1999 and 2005 I spent six years of volunteer time (approximately 1,000 hours per year) serving in a leadership role on the Icograda board (two years as president elect, two years as president, and two years as past president). This involved frequent travel on six continents, with my often being away from the office and out of communication range for weeks at a time. Personally, it was a big lesson to be able to give up the control tendencies I had always exercised, and learning how to effectively inform, empower, motivate, and then trust others with things.

(OPPOSITE) "Maxim Dictum" (our working "manifesto") CLIENT: Circle (THIS PAGE) Corporate identity design for a First Nation-owned business CLIENT: TWCC Insurance Partners LP

DESIGN IS PLAY

WHAT IS THE REASON FOR THE NAME OF YOUR STUDIO?

"Play" can be understood as freedom of movement within a defined space. It can also be understood as freedom of thought within the confines of a particular problem. We believe that design is playful when it succeeds in balancing structure and fluidity, logic with emotion.

HOW LONG HAVE YOU HAD A STUDIO?

Design is Play is a creative collaboration between Angie Wang and Mark Fox, now in its fourth year. Prior to this, Mark worked under the name BlackDog for more than twenty years.

HOW MANY EMPLOYEES (FULL-TIME AND FREELANCE)?

Angie and Mark are the only employees.

HOW MANY PRINCIPALS AND EMPLOYEES ARE DESIGNERS?

We are both designers and educators. Angie is more type-and systems-oriented; Mark is more symbol-oriented.

OTHERS?

No.

DO YOU HAVE A STRATEGIST OR ACCOUNT PERSON ON STAFF?

No.

ABOUT: For the CraftForward symposium we juxtaposed two square glyphs: a circa 1909 typographer's ornament (symbolizing "craft"), and a QR code linked to the symposium website (symbolizing "forward"). In this context the QR code functions as a modern ornament, but one with embedded content.
PHOTO: Mark Serr

DESCRIBE YOUR CLIENTELE.

Our clients tend to be entrepreneurs and, as a result, they are curious, intelligent, informed, and decisive. They appreciate fine food and wine which, believe it or not, is not that great of a leap from fine typography or fine printing. Our clients appreciate nuance and quality.

ARE YOU ATTEMPTING TO BROADEN YOUR CLIENT BASE?

Always!

DO YOU SPECIALIZE? OR GENERALIZE?

We specialize in working with certain kinds of clients. They tend to be small or closely held businesses, and we work directly with the owners. The medium that we work in varies according to the particular design problem and our clients' needs.

We know how to problem-solve and how to make images and forms. As long as we understand the parameters of a given medium, our skills are typically translatable.

ARE YOU PRIMARILY PRINT OR VIRTUAL, OR BOTH?

We design for both print and screen, although we have a particular love of the tactile experience that printing (or signage) offers. Whenever possible, we do our best to deliver a sensory experience through materiality.

One example: In our work for the CCA CraftForward symposium, we combined foil stamping, letterpress printing, offset lithography, laser printing, and screen printing with a mix of substrates, including chipboard, blotter paper, newsprint, DayGlo paper, and cotton organza. While the budget was lean, we nonetheless designed a range of pieces that cumulatively created a rich experience for the symposium attendees.

WHAT PROMPTED YOU TO START A STUDIO?

We want the freedom to succeed—and to fail. We can't realize our creative vision while executing someone else's ideas.

HOW DID YOU DETERMINE WHERE YOUR STUDIO WOULD BE LOCATED?

We love living and working in San Francisco. We are in the midst of a vibrant visual, literary, culinary, and technological culture, and our work is influenced by the particularities (and peculiarities) of this culture.

We are part of a community of visual artists who made a choice to leave somewhere else to settle in the Bay Area. Some of these folks include: Bob Aufuldish (Ohio), Dennis Crowe (North Carolina), Vivienne Flesher (New York), David Lance Goines (Oregon), Steve Lyons (Massachusetts), Michael Mabry (Illinois), Jason Munn (Wisconsin), Ward Schumaker (Nebraska), and Michael Schwab (Oklahoma). Although stylistically different from our own, the work of our friends continues to inspire and challenge us.

DESCRIBE YOUR AESTHETIC, STYLISTIC (EVEN PHILOSOPHIC) APPROACH TO DESIGN.

Much of graphic design is considered ephemera, the origin of which—"ephemeron"—refers to the mayfly and its notoriously short lifespan. Our approach to design is partially driven by a desire to make the ephemeral less so: to extend the life of our work through thoughtfulness, functionality, and craft. All of this takes time, of course, and so our approach is slow, but we don't consider this a shortcoming in the least.

In an effort to craft our work, we place great emphasis on working by hand and not letting software

PRINCIPALS
**MARK FOX
ANGIE WANG**

FOUNDED
2008

LOCATION
SAN FRANCISCO, CA

EMPLOYEES
2 FULL-TIME

become the default design tool. We still hand-ink much of our work with a Rapidograph inking pen, and we relish the physicality and tempo of this process. (By contrast, we find drawing on the computer to be a simulation of drawing.) We also hand-set type from old type specimen books and shoot our own photographs for various projects. We are committed to authoring our own images whenever we can and when appropriate.

Finally, we try to utilize vendors who value traditional methods of "making." For example, New Bohemia Signs specializes in painting signs by hand; Acme Screen Printing still hand-pulls screen prints; and Dependable Letterpress lives up to the promise of its name. If we as a profession (and a society) want a robust print and craft culture, then we need to support the printers and craftspeople who are still in business. We can't blame others for the loss of printing (or books) if we ourselves don't buy print.

HOW MUCH FREEDOM DO YOU ALLOW INDIVIDUAL DESIGNERS?
We allow ourselves complete freedom.

HOW WOULD YOU DEFINE COLLABORATION AS PRACTICED IN YOUR STUDIO?
Our collaboration is fluid, and we regularly critique and edit each other's work, whether that work is visual or textual. At its most liquid, the process of collaborating yields hybridized results that surprise both of us.

COULD YOUR STUDIO GET ALONG WITHOUT YOU FOR ANY PERIOD OF TIME?
Would the Catholic Church get along without the Pope?

March Pantry packaging **PHOTO:** Kirk Amyx

ANSON MILLS

DO YOU HAVE A LONG-TERM PLAN FOR SUSTAINABILITY OR GROWTH?

The long-term plan is to find more clients who share our values. Once we find them, we will stick to them like boll weevils. (Only well-behaved boll weevils, of course.)

WHAT IS THE MOST CHALLENGING PART OF HAVING A STUDIO?

Paul Rand noted that design is a conflict between form and content, form being the problem. For those who choose to operate a design studio, this is but the first of many conflicts!

The most challenging part of running a studio is working with other people in all capacities: as co-workers, as clients, as vendors. Graphic design is not a solitary pursuit but a collaborative one, and opportunities for miscommunication (and conflict) are legion.

DESCRIBE THE MOST SATISFYING PROJECT(S) OF THE PAST YEAR.

Anson Mills of Columbia, South Carolina is unique in contemporary food culture: They specialize in growing, harvesting, and cold-milling organic heirloom grains—all dating from the antebellum South and bred exclusively for flavor. They are zealously committed to regional authenticity and to the resuscitation and repatriation of near-extinct varieties of corn, rice, and wheat.

We are honored to work with Anson Mills, and we proudly serve their grains to our children. To date we have redesigned the Anson Mills identity and packaging system, and we are currently at work on a redesign of their website.

(TOP & MIDDLE) ABOUT: Our original sketch using hand-traced type for an invitation to be screen-printed on a Tyvek apron. The sketch is 3½ inches wide, but the client liked it so much that it became the basis for the final 23 x 35 inch piece. **CLIENT:** March Pantry **PHOTO:** Mark Serr **(BOTTOM)** Anson Mills identity

PRINCIPAL
EDUARD ČEHOVIN

FOUNDED
1988

LOCATION
**LJUBLJANA,
SLOVENIA**

EMPLOYEES
1 FULL-TIME

DESIGN CENTER LTD.

WHAT IS THE REASON FOR THE NAME OF YOUR STUDIO?

There is no real reason for the name of the studio. Basically, it derives from the general field in which we practice. In the long term, my vision is for the studio to evolve into a real design center with its own specific characteristics.

HOW LONG HAVE YOU HAD A STUDIO?

Under different names, in various countries, with changing currencies, under unstable regimes, and with different wives, since 1988.

HOW MANY EMPLOYEES (FULL-TIME AND FREELANCE)?

Design Center is a studio for custom-made visual communication projects. As the head and owner of the studio and the only one constantly working in the studio itself, I have the privilege of choosing challenging design projects. I am always the art director and creative director, but depending on the complexity of the design, the staff can be enlarged with freelance-specific design profiles. In the studio, there are no permanent full-time or freelance employees. I am employed full-time at the Academy of Fine Arts and Design, University of Ljubljana.

HOW MANY PRINCIPALS AND EMPLOYEES ARE DESIGNERS?

The only permanent designer in the studio is myself. All the other designers come and go along with the projects.

OTHERS?

Generally speaking I am "home alone."

DO YOU HAVE A STRATEGIST OR ACCOUNT PERSON ON STAFF?

As an extra small and "mobile" studio, we are in no position and have no need to hire a professional strategist. I have been working for many global advertising agencies, among them McCann-Erickson, Saatchi & Saatchi, Ogilvy & Mather, and I have learned from the inside how the big systems strategically work. From that derives my decision to work on large-scale projects like movies. Each time I choose, depending on the context and "characters" of the project, associates capable of making the project successful.

DESCRIBE YOUR CLIENTELE.

Nice and determined CEOs who believe and trust that my design can help them to improve their corporate politics.

ARE YOU ATTEMPTING TO BROADEN YOUR CLIENT BASE?

Due to the fact that I am employeed full-time as a professor at the University of Ljubljana, I have the privilege and luck to selectively choose clients and projects. I intend to continue to do that also in the future.

DO YOU SPECIALIZE? OR GENERALIZE?

I specialize in interesting and intriguing design projects.

ARE YOU PRIMARILY PRINT OR VIRTUAL, OR BOTH?

Generally speaking, as a previous-century human, I am a print media designer. But, as a this-century human, I do understand the needs of the world around us, so in some cases I work on virtual projects as well.

WHAT PROMPTED YOU TO START A STUDIO?

At the time I was working for global advertising and design agencies, and I decided to initiate my own studio to work on sustainable principles, custom-made projects, and being my own boss—deciding when and with whom to have a cup of coffee.

HOW DID YOU DETERMINE WHERE YOUR STUDIO WOULD BE LOCATED?

My xxx-small studio and I are like a snail. I live in Ljubljana, Slovenia, and so does my tiny studio.

DESCRIBE YOUR AESTHETIC, STYLISTIC (EVEN PHILOSOPHIC) APPROACH TO DESIGN.

I am constantly looking for letters that are in love with my work.

ABOUT: To commemorate the hundredth anniversary of the birth of Slovenian avant-garde poet Srecko Kosovel (1904-1926), with the help of the company Metropolis, I designed a project titled "SK04." The project encompasses my own visual interpretation of selected Kosovel poems from the collection *Integrals*. This collection is an example of so-called concrete or visual poetry. All of the billboards appeared on the corner of Slovenska Street and Askerceva Street in Ljubljana. From January to May all poems were presented at the same time at the same location.

HOW MUCH FREEDOM DO YOU ALLOW INDIVIDUAL DESIGNERS?

As an individual and, most of the time, the only designer in the studio, the freedom is sometimes more of an obstacle; self-restriction is needed for the job to get done.

HOW WOULD YOU DEFINE COLLABORATION AS PRACTICED IN YOUR STUDIO?

Collaboration is always easy and smooth, since I am the only one to make all relevant decisions.

COULD YOUR STUDIO GET ALONG WITHOUT YOU FOR ANY PERIOD OF TIME?

The studio is where I lay my head with my laptop under my arm. But that works only for a shorter period of time.

DO YOU HAVE A LONG-TERM PLAN FOR SUSTAINABILITY OR GROWTH?

My long-term plan for sustainability is imposing more strongly sustainable aspects on the studio space and its activity. In the future I plan to stay a custom-made project design studio.

WHAT IS THE MOST CHALLENGING PART OF HAVING A STUDIO?

The most thrilling part is being and working in a warm, domestic environment.

DESCRIBE THE MOST SATISFYING PROJECT(S) OF THE PAST YEAR.

Actually I am still working on this project. It is a long-term design project on which I am working for a year and a half. It is going to be finished sometime next year.

ABOUT: Starting (building) a "new life" from scratch, with a new job and a new house, was my main inspiration for using a brick as a Christmas card (and, moreover, a brick has six surfaces).

FELIX SOCKWELL, INC

WHAT IS THE REASON FOR THE NAME OF YOUR STUDIO?

In case I go broke, the bank can't take my house [where my studio is located]. The house goes to my wife, who, after getting yelled at for nearly taking a job as a Fox News personality, is divorcing this idiot. "It's just like the *Today Show*," she said. My head exploded into my pasta, which I ate the next morning, while sobbing.

HOW LONG HAVE YOU HAD A STUDIO?

I have been drawing icons and logos as an art director since 1991. I began illustrating in 1999 full time. In 1997 I moved from Texas to San Francisco, where I met Brian Collins. We then flew to New York to form BIG, then I flew that coop a year later. (Side note: The reason I left was due to a dispute over a design Louise Fili penned for a female-owned soy-based product we were developing for Unilever. In the focus group, one woman blurted, "Who designed this shit? A bunch of MEN?" My co-worker (Thomas Vasquez) was with me in the next room eating pizza, and Pepsi shot through his nose. Anyway, I had fought Brian for a week to include this Fili design as part of the proposal. It was conservative but tasteful. I thought it needed to be shown. As it happened, this was the only design (of twenty) the focus group women found agreeable. I yelled at Brian and was rewarded with an empty box and a one-way ticket down the escalator.)

HOW MANY EMPLOYEES (FULL-TIME AND FREELANCE)?

Just me. I try to promote myself as a collaborative person. Sometimes I generate ideas. Sometimes I polish ideas.

Both are enjoyable. I just go with it.

DO YOU HAVE A STRATEGIST OR ACCOUNT PERSON ON STAFF?

No. I sometimes outsource large jobs to strategists or executives if I feel nervous or need a buffer between the client and myself.

Sometimes clients ask to negotiate with a third party. I like this because it means they actually have money.

DESCRIBE YOUR CLIENTELE.

Most of my clients are out of jobs, so I do a good deal of free work. And yard work.

ARE YOU ATTEMPTING TO BROADEN YOUR CLIENT BASE?

Definitely. I've been doing GUI a lot. It's boring as hell. Like typography design but with isotopes. No one even knows what an isotope is, but I say it in meetings a lot to confuse people and make it sound like I know what I'm doing.

But seriously, there's a real need for function in what we do as designers. Visuals need to be useful. People stare at phones, not brochures. You have less time and space to communicate.

DO YOU SPECIALIZE? OR GENERALIZE?

That's a tough one to answer. I really do both. I like to jump in with the agency and help write, then work up tags and storyboards and packaging and icons and animation. Anything but HTML. If it's four letters, starts with an *H* and ends with an *L*, you're gonna get burned.

ARE YOU PRIMARILY PRINT OR VIRTUAL, OR BOTH?

I used to be print. Clients are rethinking their media buys and year

PRINCIPAL
FELIX SOCKWELL

FOUNDED
1999

LOCATIONS
**NEW JERSEY,
NEW YORK**

EMPLOYEES
1 FULL-TIME

New York Times Graphical User Interface
CREATIVE DIRECTOR/ART DIRECTOR: Caryn Tutino and Khoi Vinh

by year, print is losing. Pretty soon everything will be virtual, and I have to say I like this notion. Less paper = more trees.

WHAT PROMPTED YOU TO START A STUDIO?

When I quit my job at Ogilvy I had nothing. Nowhere to go. My friend (and roommate) Erik Johnson encouraged me to do what he was doing: illustrating. I had my reservations, but I tried it out. I supplemented my income by stealing one of Paula Scher's clients: Le Hotel Parker Meridien on Fifty-Seventh Street. I just went to the library, picked out a Red Book, went through the names of CEOs and CMOs at Hotels, mailed out a one-page form letter, and eventually ended up with Loews and Le Meridien. After a year my illustration practice was booming, and the rest is history. Right now is another transitional period where I'm retooling what I do. I've been doing animations for the World Health Org/UNITAID and some branding things. I've also been teaching art to kindergarteners.

HOW DID YOU DETERMINE WHERE YOUR STUDIO WOULD BE LOCATED?

I tell people I have two studios; one here in Maplewood, NJ, the other in Manhattan, at Thirty-Fifth and Eighth (Starbucks).

DESCRIBE YOUR AESTHETIC, STYLISTIC (EVEN PHILOSOPHIC) APPROACH TO DESIGN.

One of my favorite collaborators is Jerry Kuyper, who designed the original AT&T mark under Saul Bass. He described me as "the laziest designer in history. So lazy, he never picks up his pen." It's true. My aesthetic is "get it done." Fast. But here's the thing: What looks "fast and easy" probably took me twenty years to distill. I go deep into

the rabbit hole on important, tough assignments and end up with tons of scrap for the next, easy job. It may seem lazy to recycle too often, but you have to think like a used car salesman. Be smart. Don't waste energy. Some customers just want to buy an old muffler.

HOW WOULD YOU DEFINE COLLABORATION AS PRACTICED IN YOUR STUDIO?

Everything is a collaboration. This means you have to be able to act in different roles. As a salesperson and negotiator (initially), then creatively. Some people need to hear it AND see it. Young people don't realize the importance of justifying your decision-making process. You have to constantly rationalize.

DO YOU HAVE A LONG-TERM PLAN FOR SUSTAINABILITY OR GROWTH?

What am I? A hedge fund? No. Growth is always about failure. If you can sustain being a failure, you're going to make out well, eventually.

WHAT IS THE MOST CHALLENGING PART OF HAVING A STUDIO?

For me, billing, babysitting the kids while I work, mowing the yard, and feeding the birds, rabbits, dog, and turtles. I also have a few bullfrogs in the pond that need help with raccoons. Other than that, updating software and hardware is a constant pain.

DESCRIBE THE MOST SATISFYING PROJECT(S) OF THE PAST YEAR.

Satisfying? Well, I'd have to say the UNITAID animation is rewarding because we are actually helping to save the lives of kids in Africa (UNITAID delivers meds for TB, malaria, and AIDS). The client basically handed me six figures and told me to find an animation house. That's trust! Freedom and trust are huge creative boosts.

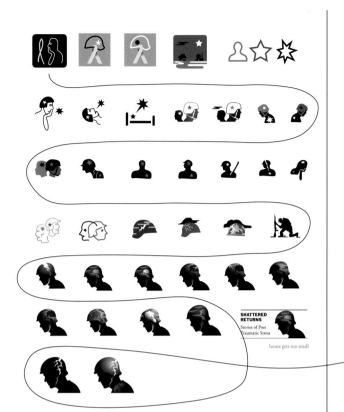

SHATTERED RETURNS
Stories of Post Traumatic Stress

house gets too small

War Torn
A series of articles and multimedia about veterans of the wars in Iraq and Afghanistan who have committed killings, or been charged with them, after coming home.

DD: Margaret O'Connor
New York Times

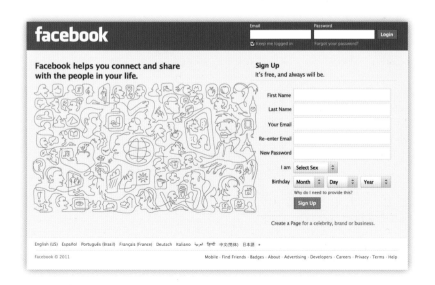

(TOP) War Torn **DESIGN DIRECTOR:** Margaret O'Connor **CLIENT:** New York Times **(LEFT AND FOLLOWING SPREAD) CLIENT:** Facebook **DESIGN DIRECTOR:** Ji Lee **ART DIRECTOR:** Ben Barry **ILLUSTRATOR:** Felix Sockwell

DONDINA ASSOCIATI

WHAT IS THE REASON FOR THE NAME OF YOUR STUDIO?

Dondina is my last name, and the *associati* (associates) are my partners. Right from the start I thought it would be useful for the studio to be affiliated with my name, giving the business a strong, highly personal identity. This decision has occasionally focused too much attention on my personal role, but on the plus side it has also made us more clearly recognizable and given clients a strong sense of our solid, individualized reliability.

HOW LONG HAVE YOU HAD A STUDIO?

We opened in 1986, so the studio is turning twenty-five this year. It's our silver anniversary.

HOW MANY EMPLOYEES (FULL-TIME AND FREELANCE)?

Over the years, the studio has always stayed relatively small—we're a "petite" design workshop. Even at our largest, we've never expanded beyond six associates. Right now there are three of us at the studio's core, two full-time colleagues and myself.

HOW MANY PRINCIPALS AND EMPLOYEES ARE DESIGNERS?

All of us at the studio are designers.

OTHERS?

At the end of 2009 one of our partners moved to New York, which gave us a base there and helped fortify relationships we'd already established, as well as create new ones for future opportunities.

Although Pamela returned to Milan in September 2011, so the studio no longer has a brick-and-mortar base in the city, we're still working on a few interesting collaborations with clients there.

Depending on specific projects' requirements, the studio also works with outside colleagues in various professions: designers, editors, digital processing shops, photographers, and translators.

DO YOU HAVE A STRATEGIST OR ACCOUNT PERSON ON STAFF?

The strategy, business plan, and administration are all part of what I oversee, and consultants assist us with the financial and contractual details.

DESCRIBE YOUR CLIENTELE.

Our clientele primarily consists of medium- to large-scale companies, museums, art galleries, cultural institutions, and publishers.

Because we're based in Milan, we've had the good fortune of working with various firms in the fashion and design worlds, two of Italy's top fields. Some of our most long-term clients include Giorgio Armani, Valentino, Ferragamo, Cassina, and others—brands that are recognized worldwide and have helped export the "Made in Italy" phenomenon.

ARE YOU ATTEMPTING TO BROADEN YOUR CLIENT BASE?

We're always looking to strengthen our position and expand our clientele, especially abroad.

PRINCIPAL
FRANCESCO DONDINA

FOUNDED
1986

LOCATIONS
MILAN & NEW YORK

EMPLOYEES
3 FULL-TIME

Right now our newest clients include an art gallery in Paris, the Victoria Morell Gallery, and the Asia Society Museum in New York. Things are a bit stagnant in Italy at the moment. The financial crisis has drastically reduced both private companies' and public institutions' investments in comunication; museums and other cultural institutions are getting a lot less government funding than they used to.

DO YOU SPECIALIZE? OR GENERALIZE?

I'd say our work covers all design-related fields, although most of our projects fall into the sectors of branding/corporate identity and book design.

The sectors we do the least work in are packaging and retail design.

ARE YOU PRIMARILY PRINT OR VIRTUAL, OR BOTH?

Our work is done in both the print and digital realms.

We design and implement websites for our clients, of course, but we're most closely tied to ink-on-paper products. Books are what we love to create most. In addition to the layout, deciding on the right materials—the right paper, the right format—and working on the overall book object are all parts of a process we find infinitely intriguing.

Over the last few months we've begun looking into e-publishing and the visual interfaces of apps and other publishing sectors, but we're still in the developmental phase there. We're working on it—that's the future.

WHAT PROMPTED YOU TO START A STUDIO?

I was pretty young when I founded the studio.

Back then, I was just a twenty-four-year-old kid with an undeniable passion for the trade, a healthy dose

of audacity, and a strong entrepreneurial spirit.

Now that I'm twice that age, I'm basically the same—the sole difference being that I've made a lot of mistakes, which has made me grow up.

I'd say passion, chutzpah, and an enterprising drive are necessary ingredients for anyone thinking about opening their own studio, at any age.

HOW DID YOU DETERMINE WHERE YOUR STUDIO WOULD BE LOCATED?

Milan is a small city. It might not be as beautiful or historic as other Italian cities, but it's a town where you can get down to work without being too distracted by the country's stunning landscapes, amazing artistic masterpieces, and the quintessential Italian flair for *la dolce vita*.

Anyone born in the heart of Milan, as I was, really can't deny the draw of its gray streets, its unique nineteenth-century neighborhoods, its hidden courtyards, and its secret gardens.

My studio is in the quiet courtyard of an old building in Milan's historic center, between the main canal and the Basilica of Sant'Ambrogio, the city's oldest.

It's a former workshop, with high ceilings and light-filled windows overlooking the courtyard. It has a few defects—it's hot in the summer and cold in the winter, and could probably use a thorough renovation—but I've never wanted to whitewash its original artisanal character.

We've been there for twenty-five years and it's a locus for our clients and friends, who like stopping by to enjoy the spot's singular silence and calm.

Maybe I'm a bit old-fashioned or spoiled, but I really can't get behind the idea of moving farther out; I don't believe in the "diffuse city" and urban sprawl, and I'm not attracted to formerly industrial areas that have gentrified into areas full of chichi, cookie-cutter lofts that take fifteen subway stops or an hour by car to get to.

Aside from our international clients, most of our clientele is here in central Milan, so for me it's perfectly natural that we'd stay put.

DESCRIBE YOUR AESTHETIC, STYLISTIC (EVEN PHILOSOPHIC) APPROACH TO DESIGN.

We believe that design—and communication design in particular—is a discipline that brings together a humanist grounding, functionalist rigor, visual and textual responsibility, and the incessant quest for new forms of language.

When we begin a new project, from paper to pixel, we treat it as a creative problem to be analyzed from every point of view. We look for solutions, but we also aspire to go beyond them, to find the best possible alternatives.

We've never aimed to astonish; rather, we like to understand everything we give visual form to—every bit of info, every detail, every message, every thought process—and make it comprehensible and coherent as a whole.

We aren't obsessed with style; rather, we pursue and are absolutely faithful to the idea of a pared-down, rigorous sensibility—a taste that I'd say is typically Milanese. If you were to distill the design ethos of this city into a single term, it'd be "sober elegance."

That's why we unwaveringly honor and respect the laws of synthesis and the search for simplicity, because—as Brancusi said—simplicity isn't simple; rather, it's the solution of complexity.

Figure del Mare **ABOUT:** For Mimmo Jodice at the Museo di Fotografia Contemporanea in Milan

MIA
Milan Image Art Fair

Corporate identity of MIA, the Milan Image Art Fair

HOW MUCH FREEDOM DO YOU ALLOW INDIVIDUAL DESIGNERS?

The greatest possible freedom, within the bounds of the design principles and stylistic sense outlined above.

HOW WOULD YOU DEFINE COLLABORATION AS PRACTICED IN YOUR STUDIO?

I'd use the term "sharing."

My colleagues and I are a team, a group in which every single person has a precise role and carries out a given number of works independently while following the work of others within our shared practice. My specific role goes beyond the task of design, and that's what shapes the guidelines and spirit of the various phases of any given project, from the initial idea to its final production. Everything is done in the spirit of sharing and open comparison and encounter.

I'm convinced that's the right way to make each and every design coming from our studio truly effective and recognizable.

COULD YOUR STUDIO GET ALONG WITHOUT YOU FOR ANY PERIOD OF TIME?

The studio is self-sufficient and works perfectly well when I'm physically absent, thanks to its detailed internal organization, the proper subdivision of responsibilities, and everyone's mutual trust.

That said, I'm never away for more than ten days in a row, so in a way I'm always around, even in absentia. I'm a bit of a homebody in that sense.

DO YOU HAVE A LONG-TERM PLAN FOR SUSTAINABILITY OR GROWTH?

Up until a few years ago, the studio stayed afloat thanks to careful planning and a mixture of medium- and long-term commissions. The crisis that's taken hold in recent years has changed things, in the Western

world at least, quite significantly. There's a lot more instability, not only in the material aspects of the trade, but also in many relationships and the timeframe required to complete projects—things have become more spread out, and sometimes intermittent. You have to learn to travel increasingly lightly, and be ever readier to respond to the nervous twitches and uncertainties of our rapidly evolving world.

On the one hand, all these things destabilize our certainties—on the other, they push us to face the new challenges ahead.

WHAT IS THE MOST CHALLENGING PART OF HAVING A STUDIO?

The priceless sensation of always being free: free to create, free to make mistakes; free to try out and present new solutions, even to the most conservative clients—the worst that can happen is they might say no. Being able to afford such an opportunity on a daily basis is an unbeatable feeling.

Every day puts this freedom to the test, proving it anew.

DESCRIBE THE MOST SATISFYING PROJECT(S) OF THE PAST YEAR?

Some of our most satisfying projects from this past year include: the corporate identity of the Victoria Morell Gallery (Paris), the book Figure del mare for Mimmo Jodice, a major photographer whose work was shown at the Museo di Fotografia Contemporanea (Cinisello Balsamo), the annual report and company profile of the Azienda Trasporti Milanesi (City Transit Authority, Milan), the overall branding and look of MIA—the Milan Image Art Fair—Italy's first international art fair dedicated to photography and video art. But our best project always has and always will be the one we'll do tomorrow.

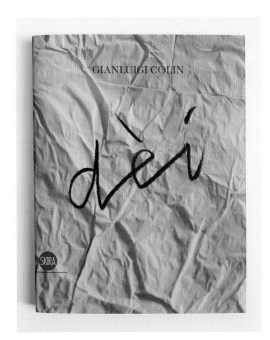

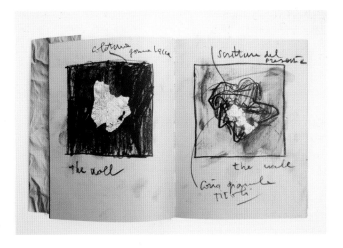

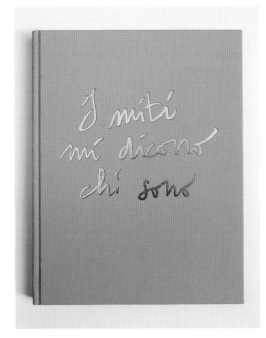

dèi, book for Gianluigi Colin, artist and art director of *Il Corriere della Sera*.

DESIGN: L'ORANGE

WHAT IS THE REASON FOR THE NAME OF YOUR STUDIO?

As a solo operator, a one-man consultancy, I simply use my name as my studio name. If there's an opportunity to set a credit on a piece of work, I use "Design: L'Orange" or simply "Gerry L'Orange."

HOW LONG HAVE YOU HAD A STUDIO?

I've been a freelancer a few times in my career. This time around, since 1995.

HOW MANY EMPLOYEES (FULL-TIME AND FREELANCE)?

No employees; occasional subcontractors.

HOW MANY PRINCIPALS AND EMPLOYEES ARE DESIGNERS?

Just me.

DO YOU HAVE A STRATEGIST OR ACCOUNT PERSON ON STAFF?

No.

DESCRIBE YOUR CLIENTELE.

Varied. A university, a private school, a couple of pharmaceutical companies. I recently finished a branding project for a restaurant and another for a gift shop. An unusual project last year was a pair of outdoor banners for a downtown cathedral.

ARE YOU ATTEMPTING TO BROADEN YOUR CLIENT BASE?

Always!

DO YOU SPECIALIZE? OR GENERALIZE?

Generalize.

ARE YOU PRIMARILY PRINT OR VIRTUAL? OR BOTH?

Primarily print.

WHAT PROMPTED YOU TO START A STUDIO?

Over the years, I've been a partner in two design firms and an employee in various design offices and ad agencies, and even, before the advent of the personal computer, at a typesetting firm. It's the work I enjoy, not the business. As a one-man studio, the emphasis is on the projects.

HOW DID YOU DETERMINE WHERE YOUR STUDIO WOULD BE LOCATED?

For the past ten years my studio has been on the ground floor of the townhouse that my wife and I own alongside Montreal's historic Lachine Canal. The studio is a five-second commute from the breakfast table. I work at home—*j'ai mon bureau à domicile*—because I'm able to.

DESCRIBE YOUR AESTHETIC, STYLISTIC (EVEN PHILOSOPHIC) APPROACH TO DESIGN.

The first order of business is of course the communication. "Is this document communicating its essence effectively?" is the question I ask myself as I work. I always bear in mind what a writer I worked with a long time ago told me: "You make my words look more convincing." After effectiveness come style, tone, grace, voice, manner, and so on. I allow the parameters of the project to influence the appropriate stylistic attributes,

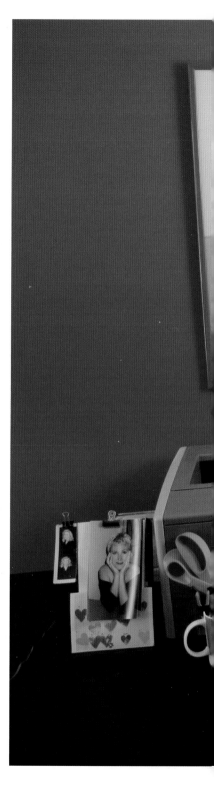

PRINCIPAL
GERRY L'ORANGE

FOUNDED
1995

LOCATION
MONTREAL, QUEBEC

EMPLOYEES
1 FULL-TIME

(TOP LEFT) Sign for nee.nah boutique **ABOUT:** nee.nah sells gifts, jewelry, fashion accessories, etc. The emphasis is on items that glitter and sparkle. The sign is acrylic and gold leaf. **(TOP RIGHT)** *Trans Canada Trail*, book **ABOUT:** I wrote, edited, and designed this book. It hit No. 6 on the Canadian hardcover nonfiction bestseller list. It was translated into French and both the English and French editions have been reprinted. It took me three weeks just to make the photo selection—I had to choose 160-odd images from among 1,800 by one of Canada's top five photographers. **(BOTTOM RIGHT)** Sushi Yu Mi sign **ABOUT:** This is the "Japanese hanko seal" portion of the visual identity. The niche is fresh and delicious at friendly prices. The tagline, echoing the face in the *U*, is "You'll smile too." **(BOTTOM LEFT)** Web offset reports for McGill University **ABOUT:** These are interesting (in my opinion) because they're low-budget, two-color, web-printed. On the document on the left I cropped an image of a construction site hoarding "window" so that it serves as a frame for the view within. Couldn't find a man-at-work pictogram that I liked, so I designed one myself. In the hi-res photo, the type on the right-hand cover is easily legible all the way to the red button; the dollar figure in the LLH corner of the left-hand cover is easily legible.

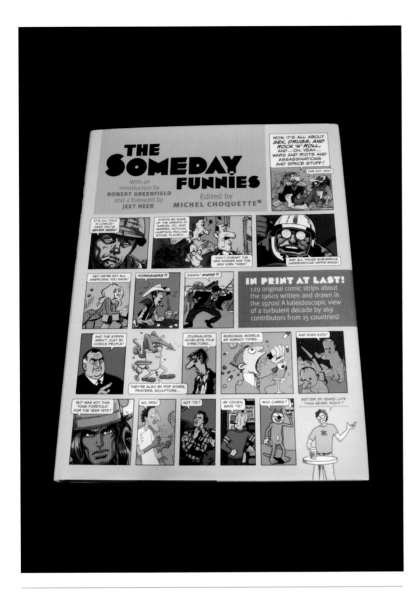

The Someday Funnies

but I always strive for simplicity. The thing has to look simple and yet striking. "Striking" not as in "Whoa, what's goin' on here?"; "Striking" as in "Over here, eyeballs; this way, attention."

COULD YOUR STUDIO GET ALONG WITHOUT YOU FOR ANY PERIOD OF TIME?

No. When I'm on holiday the studio is closed.

WHAT IS THE MOST CHALLENGING PART OF HAVING A STUDIO?

Adjusting the flow—avoiding having projects collide with each other.

DESCRIBE THE MOST SATISFYING PROJECT(S) OF THE PAST YEAR.

The Someday Funnies, a book project. Working closely with the editor, I designed this large-format book of never-before-published comics about the 1960s for Abrams ComicArts. I've loved books for as long as I can remember, and I've loved designing and presenting information ever since I first realized that these functions don't somehow happen automatically on the press. This complex book project was on my desk for almost two years. It was a big challenge and enormously satisfying.

IGARASHI STUDIO

PRINCIPAL
TAKENOBU IGARASHI

FOUNDED
1970

LOCATION
SHINTOTSUKAWA, JAPAN

EMPLOYEES
2 FULL-TIME

WHAT IS THE REASON FOR THE NAME OF YOUR STUDIO?
I wanted it to be very clear that it is my own studio.

HOW LONG HAVE YOU HAD A STUDIO?
Forty-one years.

HOW MANY EMPLOYEES (FULL-TIME AND FREELANCE)?
1970–1975: one full-time;
1976–1979: three to four full-time;
1980–1994: ten to sixteen full-time and two freelance;
1995–present: two full-time.

HOW MANY PRINCIPALS AND EMPLOYEES ARE DESIGNERS?
1970–1975: one designer;
1976–1979: three to four designers;
1980–1994: nine to fourteen designers;
1995–present: one designer.

OTHERS?
Secretary.

DO YOU HAVE A STRATEGIST OR ACCOUNT PERSON ON STAFF?
1980–1994: one strategist.

DESCRIBE YOUR CLIENTELE?
Various fields, big and small, private and public, domestic and overseas for graphic, product, sculpture, and art. Mitsui Bank, Suntory, Zanders, MoMA, Oji paper, Honda, Japan Railroad, City of San Francisco, Neocon19.

ARE YOU ATTEMPTING TO BROADEN YOUR CLIENT BASE?
No.

DO YOU SPECIALIZE? OR GENERALIZE?
Generalize.

ARE YOU PRIMARILY PRINT OR VIRTUAL? OR BOTH?
Print.

WHAT PROMPTED YOU TO START A STUDIO?
I had expected to return to Tama Art University with a Master's after studying at UCLA, but at that time, Tama was closed due to student riots. So I started my own studio in 1970.

HOW DID YOU DETERMINE WHERE YOUR STUDIO WOULD BE LOCATED?
My only choice was starting in my own apartment.

DESCRIBE YOUR AESTHETIC, STYLISTIC (EVEN PHILOSOPHIC) APPROACH TO DESIGN?
Design is discovering.

(TOP) Kazenobi ABOUT: When Yoshino Elementary School closed its doors after 103 years, the farming town of Shin-Totsukawa-cho, the neighboring town of Takikawa where I grew up, decided to restore and appropriate the school facility into my atelier and gallery. I wanted it to be a place of communication and experience through sculpture, named Kazenobi ("Beauty of the Wind"). DATE: 2011 CLIENT: Town of Shintotsukawa ARCHITECT: Yoshihiko Iida+IAS PHOTO: Machiko Endo (BOTTOM LEFT) White Legend at Kazenobi DATE: 2011 CLIENT: Town of Shintotsukawa ARCHITECT: Yoshihiko Iida+IAS PHOTO: Mitsumasa Fujitsuka ABOUT: In creating this daydream, like a breath of air intrinsic to the natural beauty of the harsh winters in my hometown, I worked on fragile light details and did all the carving and modeling by myself, finishing up with four different pale white glazes. (BOTTOM RIGHT) Takenobu Igarashi PHOTO: Shinya Fujiwara

Interior Space Graphics for Paseo at Sapporo Station **DATE:** 2011 **CLIENT:** Sapporo Station General Development Co., Ltd. **DESIGNER:** Takenobu Igarashi **ARCHITECT:** Nihon Sekkei, Inc. **PHOTO:** Mitsumasa Fujitsuka

HOW MUCH FREEDOM DO YOU ALLOW INDIVIDUAL DESIGNERS?
I listen to everyone's opinion. But I develop the concept and design by myself.

HOW WOULD YOU DEFINE COLLABORATION AS PRACTICED IN YOUR STUDIO?
Any task for success.

COULD YOUR STUDIO GET ALONG WITHOUT YOU FOR ANY PERIOD OF TIME?
Yes, for three to four months.

DO YOU HAVE A LONG-TERM PLAN FOR SUSTAINABILITY OR GROWTH?
No. I am flexible when it comes to the future.

WHAT IS THE MOST CHALLENGING PART OF HAVING A STUDIO?
Compensation.

DESCRIBE THE MOST SATISFYING PROJECT(S) OF THE PAST YEAR.
We secured creative freedom for the following projects in 2011: terra-cotta sculpture, big clock, interior and graphic design commissioned by JR (Japan Railroad) at Sapporo Station.

(TOP) Forest of "Terminus" at Sapporo Station **ABOUT:** The mystic forest inhabited by the god Terminus is a terra-cotta mural sculpture expressing my respect to the gods. **DATE:** 2011 **CLIENT:** Sapporo Station General Development Co., Ltd. **ARTIST:** Takenobu Igarashi **PHOTO:** Mitsumasa Fujitsuka (BOTTOM) Big Clock of Stars at Sapporo Station **ABOUT:** The world's largest station clock is designed to withstand earthquakes and is equipped with photovoltaic panels. **CLIENT:** Sapporo Station General Development Co., Ltd. **DATE:** 2011 **DESIGNER:** Takenobu Igarashi **ARCHITECT:** Nihon Sekkei, Inc. **MATERIAL:** Stainless steel

MELCHIOR IMBODEN

WHAT IS THE REASON FOR THE NAME OF YOUR STUDIO?
I use my name because I work mostly alone.

HOW LONG HAVE YOU HAD A STUDIO?
I started in 1991.

HOW MANY EMPLOYEES (FULL-TIME AND FREELANCE)?
I mostly work alone, unless there is a job for a museum-like exhibition design or book design. For example, for my last project, for which I won the 2011 Kieler Woche design competition, I worked together with a young designer.

HOW MANY PRINCIPALS AND EMPLOYEES ARE DESIGNERS?
They are mostly designers.

OTHERS?
For exhibition or book design I work with artists, photographers, museum directors, or historians of art.

DO YOU HAVE A STRATEGIST OR ACCOUNT PERSON ON STAFF?
No.

DESCRIBE YOUR CLIENTELE.
Art museums, galleries, theaters, music organizations, editors, and other private clients.

PRINCIPAL
MELCHIOR IMBODEN

FOUNDED
1991

LOCATION
SWITZERLAND

EMPLOYEES
1 FULL-TIME

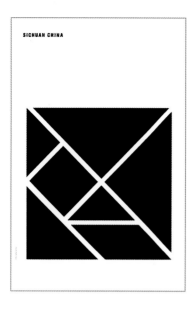

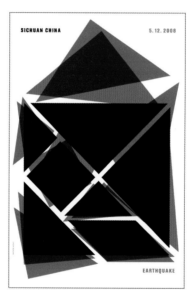

Earthquake **ABOUT:** Invitational poster
exhibition **DESIGNER:** Melchior Imboden
MEDIUM: Silk screen **SIZE:** 90.5 cm x
128 cm **(OPPOSITE)** *Melchoir Imboden
Poster Grafik* (permanent exhibiton
in Lucerne) **CLIENT:** Gallery Reussbad
Lucerne **DESIGNER:** Melchior Imboden
MEDIUM: Silk screen **SIZE:** 90.5 cm x
128 cm (series of fourteen posters)
DATE: 2009

ARE YOU ATTEMPTING TO BROADEN YOUR CLIENT BASE?

I am very happy with my situation,
namely being able to work with
cultural institutes.

DO YOU SPECIALIZE? OR GENERALIZE?

My favorite clients are based in the
cultural field.

ARE YOU PRIMARILY PRINT OR VIRTUAL, OR BOTH?

I am firmly grounded only in print. As
a photographer I do my own artwork
for books and exhibitions.

WHAT PROMPTED YOU TO START A STUDIO?

When I studied graphic design I
was the winner of two very important photo awards and a Swiss
poster award. When I completed my
studies I first started to work in the
biggest public relations agencies in
Zürich. I always wanted to be free,
and I worked for art galleries a lot
at that time. After that I started my
studio at the time when I released
my portrait photo book, *Nidwaldner
Gesichter*.

HOW DID YOU DETERMINE WHERE YOUR STUDIO WOULD BE LOCATED?

I started by working at home, because of the money. And then, ten
years ago, I moved into my father's
house. He was a farmer and died
when I was three years old. Later
a sister of mine lived there. When
she moved ten years ago to live in
another place, I decided to live and
work there. It's located very nicely
in the middle of Switzerland, making
it is easy to reach Lucerne, Zürich,
Basel, Bern, and Milan.

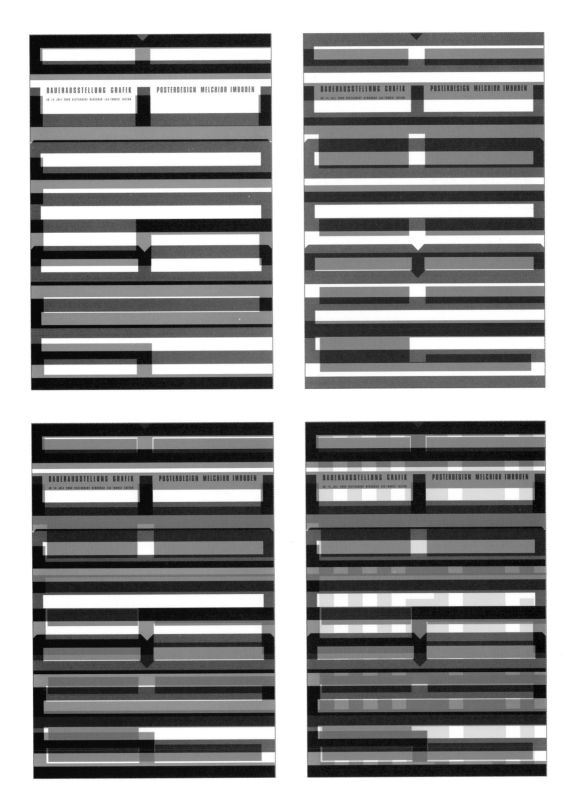

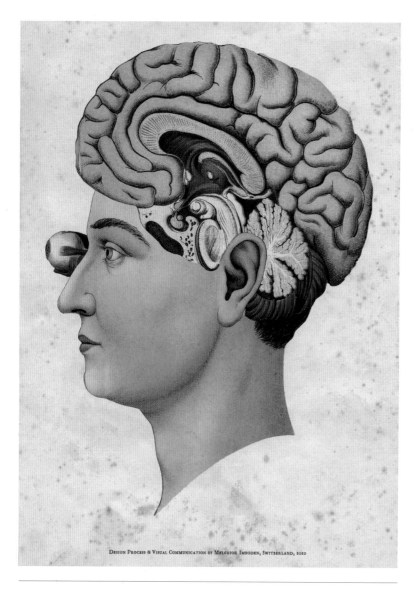

DESIGN PROCESS & VISUAL COMMUNICATION BY MELCHIOR IMBODEN, SWITZERLAND, 2010

Design Process **ABOUT:** Invitational poster exhibtion /
AGI Congress Porto **DATE:** 2010 **MEDIUM:** Offset print
SIZE: 90.5 cm x 128 cm

DESCRIBE YOUR AESTHETIC, STYLISTIC (EVEN PHILOSOPHIC) APPROACH TO DESIGN?

My favorite style is a typographic, often reduced style, which can often be connected with photography.

HOW MUCH FREEDOM DO YOU ALLOW INDIVIDUAL DESIGNERS?

I think a good designer should have an enormous amount of freedom.

HOW WOULD YOU DEFINE COLLABORATION AS PRACTICED IN YOUR STUDIO?

I work mostly alone in my studio.

COULD YOUR STUDIO GET ALONG WITHOUT YOU FOR ANY PERIOD OF TIME?

No. I have to get everything organized myself before leaving the studio to visit another country for a workshop, jury, or an exhibition.

DO YOU HAVE A LONG-TERM PLAN FOR SUSTAINABILITY OR GROWTH?

I always have to work and do a lot of organizing, even at night.

WHAT IS THE MOST CHALLENGING PART OF HAVING A STUDIO?

Managing my time at work in between stretches of free time.

DESCRIBE THE MOST SATISFYING PROJECT(S) OF THE PAST YEAR.

It was a great pleasure to be the winner of Kieler Woche 2011 and to work on the whole project, including posters, flyers, T-shirts, cars, and everything else in the huge spectrum of merchandise for the biggest sailing event in the world.

(TOP LEFT) 30 Years of the Ermitage Art Gallery **CLIENT:** Ermitage art gallery **MEDIUM:** Silk screen **SIZE:** 90.5 cm x 128 cm **DATE:** 2009
(TOP RIGHT) CREATIVE LOVE (Diego Rivera and Frida Kahlo) **ABOUT:** Invitational poster exhibtion **MEDIUM:** Silk screen **SIZE:** 90.5 cm x
128 cm **DATE:** 2007 (BOTTOM LEFT) KIELER WOCHE 2011 **CLIENT:** City of Kiel **MEDIUM:** Offset print **SIZE:** 90.5 cm x 128 cm **DATE:** 2011
(BOTTOM RIGHT) BLACK AND WHITE (exhibition poster) **CLIENT:** ddd Gallery Tokyo **MEDIUM:** Offset print **SIZE:** 70 x 100 cm **DATE:** 2006

JAMES VICTORE INC.

WHAT IS THE REASON FOR THE NAME OF YOUR STUDIO?
It has a nice ring to it, don't you think?

HOW LONG HAVE YOU HAD A STUDIO?
Three months after I was asked to leave design school, I began working. I worked for six or eight years as a freelance designer under my own name, until I learned the financial advantages of incorporating and added "Inc" to my name; thus I became a "studio." All in all, it has been around (gasp) twenty-five years since I began working.

HOW MANY EMPLOYEES (FULL-TIME AND FREELANCE)?
I have one full-time/freelance designer and a rotating circus of interns. I have always thought of growing larger, but the lure of independence and designing and not "managing" coupled with the financial facts of life always stopped me.

HOW MANY PRINCIPALS AND EMPLOYEES ARE DESIGNERS?
We are all designers. I like the input of smart, funny people around me. Even the interns get to read the brief and contribute suggestions. Everyone pulls an oar around here.

DO YOU HAVE A STRATEGIST OR ACCOUNT PERSON ON STAFF?
I wish! This may be the one missing link in my work life. I never met the right person to run that end of the business; ergo, I do it myself. I am good at the job, but it is not what I am made for. And I cannot devote myself fully to the task because of the workload in the studio. I foresee this job being filled one day, but right now I am the salesman et al.

DESCRIBE YOUR CLIENTELE.
I work with brave, smart comrades who have American greenbacks and lovely euros and an occasional yen.

ARE YOU ATTEMPTING TO BROADEN YOUR CLIENT BASE?
We already have an exceptionally wide client base. We are making design, films, product, and occasionally a few illustrations. I enjoy being busy, and I love my job. I am always on the lookout for interesting folks to collaborate with. Sometimes we find them, other times they seek us out.

DO YOU SPECIALIZE? OR GENERALIZE?
I never want to get too good at anything. We work hard in a number of directions and are always searching for new and fresh marks on the page. I never want the work to look too slick or professional. I think real human beings, our audience, can smell the difference. I could not imagine doing one thing, or working within one thin ray of this glorious business.

ARE YOU PRIMARILY PRINT OR VIRTUAL, OR BOTH?
Print, film, and interactive. We are open-minded and are trying to use all media to get our point across. Although I must admit I love print. And I love making large posters that print

PRINCIPAL
JAMES VICTORE

FOUNDED
1987

LOCATION
NEW YORK, NY

EMPLOYEES
2 FULL-TIME, 1 FREELANCE

PHOTOS: Leigh Anna Thompson

in the thousands and stand erect in the street, awaiting unsuspecting citizens.

WHAT PROMPTED YOU TO START A STUDIO?
Life. Life and Love. Life and Love and Poetry. Those three things. And money, too. Life, Love, Poetry, and getting paid for it. Dang, what a happy guy am I.

HOW DID YOU DETERMINE WHERE YOUR STUDIO WOULD BE LOCATED?
Originally I liked the idea of Paris, but the commute to work everyday from NYC would have been a bitch, so instead, I started the studio in my apartment. Now it is called a "live/work." I have always lived and worked in or close by to my studio. I like this setup. It allows me a level of freedom I have always wanted. I like being able to spend time with my family, take vacations when needed, or take an occasional morning or day off to run, surf or go shoot something. The nine-to-five idea gives me hives.

DESCRIBE YOUR AESTHETIC, STYLISTIC (EVEN PHILOSOPHIC) APPROACH TO DESIGN.
These days we describe our work in more philosophic terms. First, when I started out at twenty-two, I had a job. I worked hard for years, trying to make images and marks that only I could make, to come up with ideas that were mine, but got others excited. This led to a career. This career started me teaching and took me around the world and gave me access to other people with interesting ideas. I grew and got smarter and older. Then one day, I found myself floundering, searching for meaning, and realized I had lost sight of my goals. I had no goal for the future. It took a few years to figure this out, but recently I found my reason for being

Celebrate Columbus **PHOTO:** Library of Congress **DATE:** 1992

SVA Beach Family **PHOTO:** Stock photo **GRAFITTI:** Matthew McGuinness

in this business—and a renewed joy and love of the work. So, now, instead of a job, or a career, I have a calling. I love my job and I want others, both designers and our audience, to share this love of ideas and images and words. So, to me, design is less about what the work looks like than what it says. We are content generators as much as designers. And, more importantly, the accountability we have for it.

HOW MUCH FREEDOM DO YOU ALLOW INDIVIDUAL DESIGNERS?

It is all about freedom. My clients come to us because we allow ourselves a maximum amount of elbow room and this shows in the work. A huge part of the freedom comes from the lifestyle we have chosen here in the studio. We eat nice lunches, rarely work too late and always have a pleasant atmosphere buzzing along.

HOW WOULD YOU DEFINE COLLABORATION AS PRACTICED IN YOUR STUDIO?

Design is a collaborative business. Collaboration and compromise. As much as I want to be a diva and impose my own brand of "the truth" and imperialism on the world, we collaborate and compromise.

COULD YOUR STUDIO GET ALONG WITHOUT YOU FOR ANY PERIOD OF TIME?

Not at the moment, but we are working on that as I speak. I have a razor sharp designer in my studio now, Chris Thompson, who is helping me frame the future in an interesting fashion.

DO YOU HAVE A LONG-TERM PLAN FOR SUSTAINABILITY OR GROWTH?

Yes. I have new goals (as mentioned earlier) that take me and the studio into the year 2032. Through

Homme A/W 2008-09

(TOP) Yohji Poster **(LEFT)** Hero Platter
PHOTO: Tom Schierlitz

work, my regular teaching gig at the School of Visual Arts, and workshops with my droogs Paul Sahre and Jan Wilker (Sahre Victore Wilker), and even my own workshop (The Dinner Series), I will continue to grow and share and expand this little pirate ship of a studio we now have into a bigger, stronger vessel.

WHAT IS THE MOST CHALLENGING PART OF HAVING A STUDIO?

One thing about having a small studio like mine is always managing cash flow. We keep a low overhead to allow us some flexibility and freedom, but at the same time we don't get as many of the larger jobs that tend to go to big, clumsy studios and agencies. I never wanted a "boutique" studio, but I guess that is the territory we have wandered into.

DESCRIBE THE MOST SATISFYING PROJECT(S) OF THE PAST YEAR.

We did a beautiful project with Biber Architects recently for the City of New York Department of Probation. We designed signage and identity for this city agency, along with five large "faux-real" motivational posters. We not only designed but wrote these inspirational/decorative works. We also just collaborated with the fashion hero and icon Yohji Yamamoto and designed a line of T-shirts for him. We are also involved in designing an exhibition identity and book for the Breda Museum in Holland. So, you see, we have a number of ways to make ourselves happy and reach a large audience.

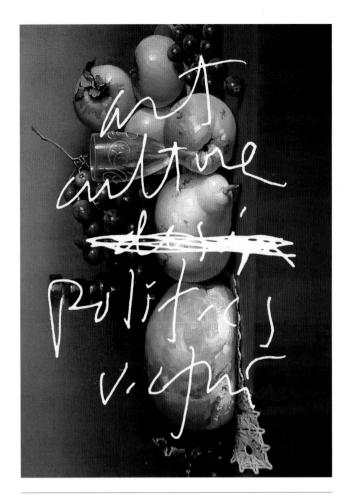

Dinner Series Postcard **IMAGE:** Public domain

EL JEFE DESIGN

WHAT IS THE REASON FOR THE NAME OF YOUR STUDIO?

It was what my wife would jokingly call me. It comes from "Jeff E.," my first name and last initial. It also is Spanish for "the boss" or "the man." I liked it because it sounded regal and important with a dash of mystery but in the end, it's just an inside joke.

I don't go by "El Jefe." I hate when I get credited as "El Jefe." And I am constantly referred to as "El Jeffy." I formally go by "Jeffrey Everett" of "El Jefe Design" but man, doesn't that sound pompous? It may not have been the best choice if I wanted to be taken as a "serious" firm, but it suits the people I want to work with.

HOW LONG HAVE YOU HAD A STUDIO?

El Jefe Design has been running for about seven years, first as a side freelance gig, now a full-time goliath.

HOW MANY EMPLOYEES (FULL-TIME AND FREELANCE)?

I am the only full-time person. I count my wife, Kelly and two sons, Max and Alex as honorary creative director and creative consultants, respectively.

I have two screen printers that I use for everything and most likely get paid more than I do.

HOW MANY PRINCIPALS AND EMPLOYEES ARE DESIGNERS?

I fill all roles, which makes it hard to yell at someone when something goes wrong.

PRINCIPAL
JEFFREY EVERETT

FOUNDED
2004

LOCATION
MARYLAND

EMPLOYEES
1 FULL-TIME

Transit U.S. Tour Poster **DESIGNER/ILLUSTRATOR:** Jeffrey Everett/El Jefe Design **PRINTER:** Team Eight **CLIENT:** Transit

OTHERS?

Do the three cats who chase bugs count?

DO YOU HAVE A STRATEGIST OR ACCOUNT PERSON ON STAFF?

No. I do have an accountant that I check in with three to four times a year as well as for taxes. I advise any designer to find an accountant and lawyer!

DESCRIBE YOUR CLIENTELE.

I mostly work with musicians and their managers. They are all creative in their fields and want something professional and lasting. They want someone who will respect what they do and will create something they can look at for the rest of their lives. Some of them are demanding and want to oversee every little detail. Some are easygoing and hire me because they know I will do a good job sight-unseen. I consider the majority of them to be friends and people whom I respect beyond being clients.

I am really lucky; I never complain about who I work with.

ARE YOU ATTEMPTING TO BROADEN YOUR CLIENT BASE?

Always! I have some great clients but like to be challenged. I don't do as many websites as I would like. That is a field I enjoy. But I get paid to draw an interpretation of music I love for eight to ten hours a day—how awesome is that?

DO YOU SPECIALIZE? OR GENERALIZE?

I am mostly known for doing graphic art for CD packaging, music posters, and merchandise. I specialize because that is what people are asking of me, but I love doing it all. I am openly pursuing more web design projects, as I feel that is a field I can

excel in. I have finished my first game app, called "Vocabador," which has been getting great press and was recently featured by Apple.

ARE YOU PRIMARILY PRINT OR VIRTUAL, OR BOTH?

Print. I love print. The web is nice, I touch in that field on occasion, but it is wonderful to see people react to the work in person. They touch the paper, hold the piece at various angles; some (like me) even enjoy smelling the ink. It is hard to frame a website or hold it up for your favorite singer to sign.

WHAT PROMPTED YOU TO START A STUDIO?

The fact that I worked at so many places and kept saying to myself, "I can do this better." I like knowing that all the responsibility comes to me. I never liked having to water down my work by showing it to a creative director, then an account rep, then the owner, THEN the client. I like working directly with the client —explaining my thoughts and work process to make a better product at the end.

HOW DID YOU DETERMINE WHERE YOUR STUDIO WOULD BE LOCATED?

I work out of my house, so I got to choose between two rooms in the basement. Over the course of five years I have overtaken both rooms with work. I didn't pick the space more than I overran it.

DESCRIBE YOUR AESTHETIC, STYLISTIC (EVEN PHILOSOPHIC) APPROACH TO DESIGN.

I like to tell stories in my work. I want something that I can look at for an hour. I try to entertain myself, and by doing so, to entertain others. My clients are friends. I want them to

Man… or Astro-Man? **DESIGNER/ILLUSTRATOR:** Jeffrey Everett/El Jefe Design **PRINTER:** Team Eight **CLIENT:** The Black Cat

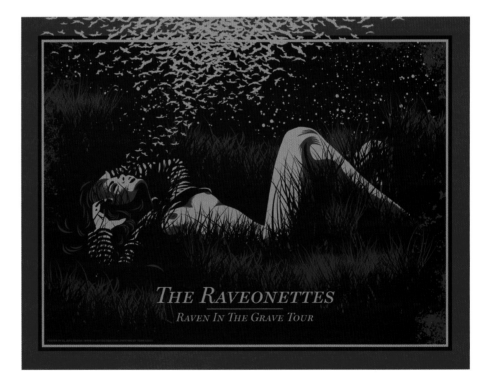

(TOP) Lou Reed 2011 UK and European Summer Tour Poster **DESIGNER/ILLUSTRATOR:** Jeffrey Everett/El Jefe Design **PRINTER:** Team Eight **CLIENT:** Lou Reed (BOTTOM) The Raveonettes - Raven in the Grave Tour Poster **DESIGNER/ILLUSTRATOR:** Jeffrey Everett/El Jefe Design **PRINTER:** Team Eight **CLIENT:** The Black Cat

have something that they are excited about and want to get behind. It is a collaboration, a partnership. I do what I feel is right—if something needs to be more "designed" and iconic, I do it. If I need to draw a hot set of boobs, I do that.

I once read about a way of thinking for music that fits with design. The author wrote there are only two types of music: good and bad. I try to do good.

HOW MUCH FREEDOM DO YOU ALLOW INDIVIDUAL DESIGNERS?
Considering it is only me, I give total freedom.

HOW WOULD YOU DEFINE COLLABORATION AS PRACTICED IN YOUR STUDIO?
Though I am the only designer, I do work closely with my printers, Team 8 and Grand Palace. I trust them implicitly. They are masters at what they do and I go to them because they can make my work look better. I hope they feel that I make the best use of their talents and create work that highlights their efforts.

COULD YOUR STUDIO GET ALONG WITHOUT YOU FOR ANY PERIOD OF TIME?
Nope. I don't think I have had a real vacation in several years. When I vacation, I know where all the free wi-fi places are, I plan work around naps and trips to the beach, and learn to not smear the screen with sunblock.

I have a wonderful and patient wife who knows I need to do work so my clients are not left hanging. When opportunity knocks, you need to be there to open the door. My clients appreciate the fact that I am there for them whenever they need me.

DO YOU HAVE A LONG-TERM PLAN FOR SUSTAINABILITY OR GROWTH?
I save money and keep things simple. I don't rent an office. I don't own the latest and greatest gadgets. I keep things simple and squirrel away money when I can. I don't do HUGE budget work, which means I need to work quickly and effectively. I usually don't turn down work unless the budget is silly or the client is wrong. I don't dick around. Time is money for me. I have been doing work that people say you cannot make money on for five years and have done well.

I keep branching out, meeting new people. I know my worth and I don't undersell myself. Head down, work hard, save money, and keep moving.

WHAT IS THE MOST CHALLENGING PART OF HAVING A STUDIO?
All the stuff that isn't design: keeping up on invoices, updating the website, all the social media, fixing the machines, making sure FedEx delivers, etc.

DESCRIBE THE MOST SATISFYING PROJECT(S) OF THE PAST YEAR.
Doing work for Lou Reed was pretty awesome and inspiring. The fact that someone so legendary and known to be difficult was thrilled by my work was such an honor. What started as just a poster turned into the identity of the entire tour—signage, backstage passes, shirts, etc. It was a pleasure to go along on that ride. Plus, getting a signed poster back was nice, especially because he put back in his one edit that was taken out—the word "fuck" written on the biker's arm.

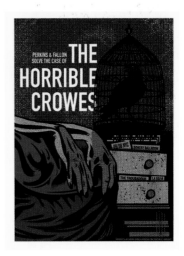

The Horrible Crowes New York/Los Angeles Concert Poster **DESIGNER/ILLUSTRATOR:** Jeffrey Everett/El Jefe Design **PRINTER:** Team Eight **CLIENT:** The Horrible Crowes

J.J. SEDELMAIER PRODUCTIONS, INC

PRINCIPALS
J.J. SEDELMAIER, PRESIDENT/DIRECTOR

PATRICE SEDELMAIER, VICE PRESIDENT/ BUSINESS MANAGER

FOUNDED
1990

LOCATION
WESTCHESTER COUNTY, NEW YORK

EMPLOYEES
4 FULL-TIME ENDLESS FREELANCE

WHAT IS THE REASON FOR THE NAME OF YOUR STUDIO?
I had built a reputation as an animation filmmaker/producer/director and wanted to be as immediately identifiable as possible. We immediately worked toward building the name into a brand. Our logo, which I designed for use on our *Saturday Night Live* "Saturday TV Funhouse" films starting in 1997, was the final stage of the process and is now well known because of the high visibility it received.

HOW LONG HAVE YOU HAD A STUDIO?
Since 1990.

HOW MANY EMPLOYEES (FULL-TIME AND FREELANCE)?
Four full-time/endless freelance.

HOW MANY PRINCIPALS AND EMPLOYEES ARE DESIGNERS?
One—yours truly.

OTHERS?
Freelance, as specific projects require. I am deeply entrenched in the illustration, cartooning, and comic book worlds, and constantly call on talent that fits the projects we're asked to produce.

DO YOU HAVE A STRATEGIST OR ACCOUNT PERSON ON STAFF?
My wife, Patrice, and I run the company together and function as both. We are regularly thinking of novel ways to promote ourselves. We solicit work that will reinforce our brand and reputation. We use film, print, editorial, and I write a bi-monthly piece for *Print* magazine's blog, *Imprint*. I also spread our gospel by speaking at schools, conventions, and advertising agencies. We're a small boutique studio with an intimate way of producing the work we do. I've found that people enjoy speaking to and hearing from the person who's directly responsible for getting their hands dirty with the work. Patrice and I also strategize constantly with our representatives.

DESCRIBE YOUR CLIENTELE.
Advertising agencies, broadcast/narrowcast networks, motion picture studios, magazines/print. We produce work in all realms of animation and design. I'm also asked to sometimes act as an ad agency co-creative director and character developer for work we ultimately don't produce.

ARE YOU ATTEMPTING TO BROADEN YOUR CLIENT BASE?
Yes. Consulting and project development are also now on our plate. We just want to involve ourselves with people and projects that are fun to work with/on, and will also support our brand—distinctive, entertaining, and often humorous.

DO YOU SPECIALIZE? OR GENERALIZE?

Generalize. We have no style but we *do* have a sensibility. Variety has been our foundation—successful work is our stamp.

ARE YOU PRIMARILY PRINT OR VIRTUAL, OR BOTH?

We're known for our animation work but have produced and created many print pieces because of my design and illustration background.

WHAT PROMPTED YOU TO START A STUDIO?

I had worked for a variety of animation studios for almost ten years, ending up at R.O. Blechman's The Ink Tank. I had worked in every capacity, from "inbetweening" (entry-level animation position) to running The Ink Tank with Blechman as executive producer/associate director and representative. Patrice and I felt we could make a go of it together—it was time.

HOW DID YOU DETERMINE WHERE YOUR STUDIO WOULD BE LOCATED?

We live in Westchester County in New York and wanted to be close to home. New York City is also very expensive to live and work in. I felt that "if we built it, they would come."

DESCRIBE YOUR AESTHETIC, STYLISTIC (EVEN PHILOSOPHIC) APPROACH TO DESIGN.

Simplicity, clarity, challenge… with an approachable, fun touch.

HOW MUCH FREEDOM DO YOU ALLOW INDIVIDUAL DESIGNERS?

As much as they require to do the project they've been brought in to do. The same courtesy I love to receive from the people we work with and for.

HOW WOULD YOU DEFINE COLLABORATION AS PRACTICED IN YOUR STUDIO?

Take a shot based upon my specs and I'll give you my feedback. I'm totally open to whatever the people I work with want to do and try, but it's my guidance and inspiration that make our work what it is so I have to have the ultimate say within the studio walls.

COULD YOUR STUDIO GET ALONG WITHOUT YOU FOR ANY PERIOD OF TIME?

Patrice and I can take a week off here and there, but otherwise, nope.

DO YOU HAVE A LONG-TERM PLAN FOR SUSTAINABILITY OR GROWTH?

We've been doing this long enough to know we want to always remain small and lean. We did the launch and first two seasons of *Beavis and Butt-Head* after being open about a year and a half. It taught us very early on that actually producing series work isn't what we're about. Managing fifty to sixty people is much different than doing work *with* eight to twelve people. A large studio is more about managing—being small is about variety and intimate involvement with the work.

WHAT IS THE MOST CHALLENGING PART OF HAVING A STUDIO?

Not being *too* busy or *too* slow, and never forgetting that everything you do should be something you want to show and share with people.

DESCRIBE THE MOST SATISFYING PROJECT(S) OF THE PAST YEAR.

We did the opening films for the Ottawa International Animation Festival—my favorite. It was an honor to be asked. The usual approach was to do an opening that the attendees would see at the beginning of each and every screening—for five days

Katrina Relief poster **CLIENT:** Katrina Poster Project **DESIGNER:** J.J. Sedelmaier **PRODUCTION/PRINTING:** Everett Studios/ Armonk NY

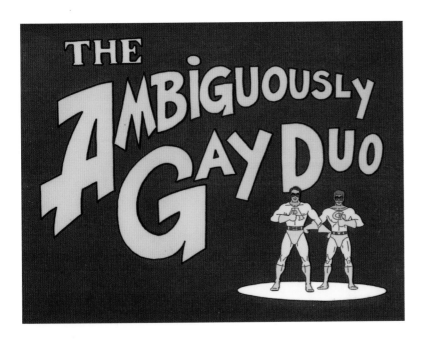

straight. No matter how good the film might be, after two, certainly three days, I would end up feeling burned out on it. I decided that we'd do a different variation for each day. You'd *think* you were going to see that same film, but then it would change and throw you off balance. After two, certainly three days, you'd wonder what was going to happen *this* time. Instead of wishing for it to finish, you'd look forward to seeing what would transpire on screen! I also was responsible for resurrecting "Speedy" Alka-Seltzer with/for Bayer and their ad agency, EnergyBBDO in Chicago. Being given the responsibility for helping to helm the reintroduction of a cultural icon was a blast. It was also an opportunity for me to demonstrate that CG (computer animation) is just another technique for making a film—telling a story. This was important because people think of us as a traditional (2D, drawn, cel) animation studio. I was then able to get *CBS News Sunday Morning* to do a segment on our work and my involvement, thus promoting the clients' work as well as JJSP.

(TOP) *The Ambiguously Gay Duo* **CREATORS:** Robert Smigel/J.J. Sedelmaier **CLIENT:** Brillstein/Grey / NBC/Universal **DESIGNER:** J.J. Sedelmaier **(BOTTOM)** "Let's Go Out to the Lobby" **CLIENT:** Fellowship Bible Church **DESIGNERS:** Dave Lovelace, Dan Madia, J.J. Sedelmaier, Claire Widman **ART DIRECTOR:** Jeff Hopfer

JOEL KATZ
DESIGN ASSOCIATES

WHAT IS THE REASON FOR THE NAME OF YOUR STUDIO?
The obvious: had just ended a partnership with a name that nobody understood and no one knew where to find me.

HOW LONG HAVE YOU HAD A STUDIO?
Since 1975. Four different names, three ex-partners, all of them wonderful people.

HOW MANY EMPLOYEES (FULL-TIME AND FREELANCE)?
One. There were fifteen of us in my second partnership studio.

HOW MANY PRINCIPALS AND EMPLOYEES ARE DESIGNERS?
One.

OTHERS?
Zero.

DO YOU HAVE A STRATEGIST OR ACCOUNT PERSON ON STAFF?
No.

DESCRIBE YOUR CLIENTELE.
Currently working on a book on information design, teaching spring semester, working in Paris/Rome half of fall semester, just finished a triannual project for an arts organization, work for the Pennsylvania Department of Transportation several times a year.

ARE YOU ATTEMPTING TO BROADEN YOUR CLIENT BASE?
No.

DO YOU SPECIALIZE? OR GENERALIZE?
Almost entirely information design, broadly defined.

ARE YOU PRIMARILY PRINT OR VIRTUAL, OR BOTH?
Print.

WHAT PROMPTED YOU TO START A STUDIO?
Got laid off.

HOW DID YOU DETERMINE WHERE YOUR STUDIO WOULD BE LOCATED?
Owned a home; had children in school; liked Philadelphia (still do).

DESCRIBE YOUR AESTHETIC, STYLISTIC (EVEN PHILOSOPHIC) APPROACH TO DESIGN.
Tell the truth; make it understandable.

HOW MUCH FREEDOM DO YOU ALLOW INDIVIDUAL DESIGNERS?
When I had them, a lot of freedom consistent with the goal above. There are always many right solutions functionally, but it helped to have a uniform style of simplicity and clarity.

PRINCIPAL
JOEL KATZ

FOUNDED
1975

LOCATION
PHILADELPHIA, PA

EMPLOYEES
1 FULL-TIME

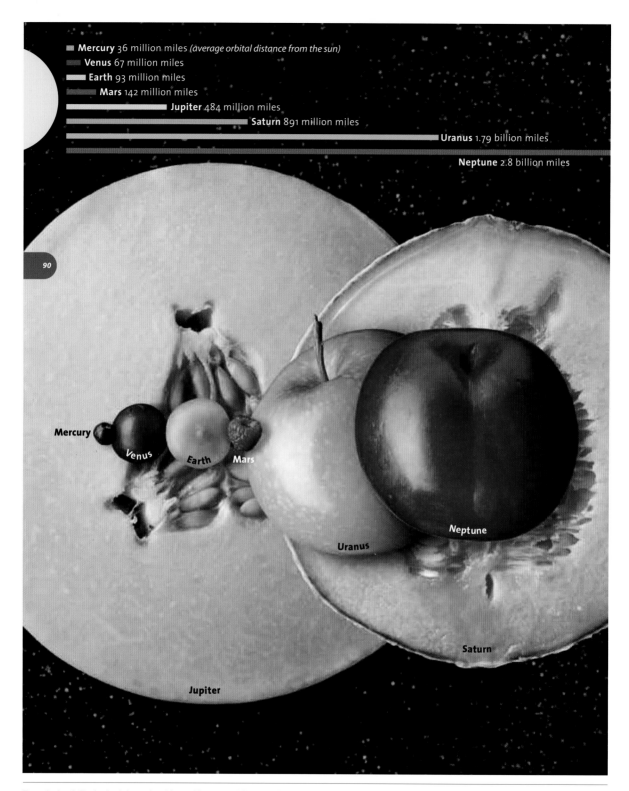

- Mercury 36 million miles *(average orbital distance from the sun)*
- Venus 67 million miles
- Earth 93 million miles
- Mars 142 million miles
- Jupiter 484 million miles
- Saturn 891 million miles
- Uranus 1.79 billion miles
- Neptune 2.8 billion miles

Mercury
Venus
Earth
Mars
Jupiter
Uranus
Neptune
Saturn

90

From the book *Designing Information: Human Factors and Common Sense in Information Design*, by Joel Katz **ABOUT:** The planets as fruit. **DESIGN:** Joel Katz
PHOTOGRAPHY: James B. Abbott **ELECTRONIC COLLAGE:** Charles Wybierala

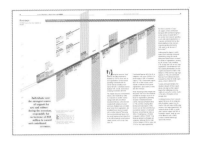

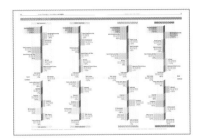

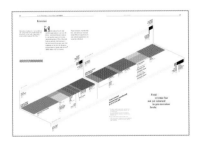

2011 Portfolio **CLIENT:** The Greater Philadelphia Cultural Alliance **DESIGN DIRECTION:** Joel Katz **DESIGN:** Mary Torrieri

HOW WOULD YOU DEFINE COLLABORATION AS PRACTICED IN YOUR STUDIO?

Principals were always open to invention by designers and studio crits were held for every project.

COULD YOUR STUDIO GET ALONG WITHOUT YOU FOR ANY PERIOD OF TIME?

Physically, absolutely.

DO YOU HAVE A LONG-TERM PLAN FOR SUSTAINABILITY OR GROWTH?

Au contraire.

WHAT IS THE MOST CHALLENGING PART OF HAVING A STUDIO?

Well, there's challenging-exciting and challenging-terrifying.

Exciting: having the opportunity to learn and to solve problems in the most appropriate and functional way, and with elegance.

Terrifying: getting the work, getting it done well and within budget, making payroll.

DESCRIBE THE MOST SATISFYING PROJECT(S) OF THE PAST YEAR.

Doing the diagrams and design for *Brand Atlas* with Alina Wheeler (former business partner); developing the concept and contents for my own book, *Designing Information: Human Factors and Common Sense in Information Design.*

KARLSSONWILKER INC.

WHAT IS THE REASON FOR THE NAME OF YOUR STUDIO?
We, Hjalti Karlsson and Jan Wilker, are the founders, and "wilkerkarlsson" didn't sound as good as "karlssonwilker." So that was it.

HOW LONG HAVE YOU HAD A STUDIO?
We started in very late 2000, so eleven years.

HOW MANY EMPLOYEES (FULL-TIME AND FREELANCE)?
These days we have four people working with us, so we're six people in here altogether.

HOW MANY PRINCIPALS AND EMPLOYEES ARE DESIGNERS?
Everyone is a designer in here.

OTHERS?
No.

DO YOU HAVE A STRATEGIST OR ACCOUNT PERSON ON STAFF?
No.

DESCRIBE YOUR CLIENTELE.
Not an easy question. Maybe they are a bit like us. We like design and we are keen on trying new things.

ARE YOU ATTEMPTING TO BROADEN YOUR CLIENT BASE?
Always.

DO YOU SPECIALIZE? OR GENERALIZE?
Both.

ARE YOU PRIMARILY PRINT OR VIRTUAL, OR BOTH?
Both.

PRINCIPALS
HJALTI KARLSSON
JAN WILKER

FOUNDED
2000

LOCATION
NEW YORK, NY

EMPLOYEES
4 FULL-TIME

Identity, signage, and wayfinding for the Museum of the Moving Image, New York. **CLIENT:** Museum of the Moving Image and Leeser Architecture **DATE:** 2011

WHAT PROMPTED YOU TO START A STUDIO?

We met at Stefan Sagmeister's studio in 1999 here in New York. When he decided to do his first sabbatical in 2000, we couldn't think of anything else to do than starting our own studio.

HOW DID YOU DETERMINE WHERE YOUR STUDIO WOULD BE LOCATED?

Eleven years ago we certainly did not overthink what could be the best location for our little studio. For us, there was only Manhattan.

We looked at around twenty spaces, and the last one we saw was perfect. We've been here ever since.

DESCRIBE YOUR AESTHETIC, STYLISTIC (EVEN PHILOSOPHIC) APPROACH TO DESIGN.

We try to have our approach change with the project at hand, from conceptual to purely formal (in regard to form), from traditional design process to erratic experimentation.

HOW MUCH FREEDOM DO YOU ALLOW INDIVIDUAL DESIGNERS?

There are projects where we are very hands-off, and there are projects where it's straightforward execution of our direction.

HOW WOULD YOU DEFINE COLLABORATION AS PRACTICED IN YOUR STUDIO?

We do not think collaboration is the answer to everything. If a project calls for it, absolutely. If not, we are more than happy to do it on our own. Overall, design should not be practiced democratically.

As far as seeing the client as a collaborator, yes, we do appreciate a client-as-collaborator relationship.

COULD YOUR STUDIO GET ALONG WITHOUT YOU FOR ANY PERIOD OF TIME?

It happens all the time that one of us

TIME magazine **ABOUT:** Year-end special twelve-page feature, including cover. **DESIGN:** karlssonwilker inc. **DESIGN & WRITING:** Jan Wilker and Hjalti Karlsson **DATE:** 2008

is or even both are out of the studio for couple of days, so, yes.

DO YOU HAVE A LONG-TERM PLAN FOR SUSTAINABILITY OR GROWTH?

No; ours is an annual "renewal of vows" between Hjalti and myself, usually in January.

WHAT IS THE MOST CHALLENGING PART OF HAVING A STUDIO?

We wouldn't have thought that design itself is only such a small fraction of what we need to be good at to run a design studio properly.

We had and still have to work very hard on ourselves to improve overall. It seems to be an endless process, this "self-improvement."

DESCRIBE THE MOST SATISFYING PROJECT(S) OF THE PAST YEAR.

- "12 Days in Jerusalem" was a project by invitation of the Israel Museum, for which we spent almost two weeks in Israel to react to each single day, visually, with a sketch/idea, on that very same day. The twelve pieces were then exhibited at the Museum with excerpts from the diary and snapshots.
- We went on an eleven-day road trip from Munich to Istanbul for MINI/BMW, in collaboration with *Matter Magazine*, together with a writer, a photographer, and a videographer. We collected interviews, impressions, dialogs, visuals, etc., trying to take the "creative temperature" of the countries we passed through on our way to Istanbul.
- New York's Museum of the Moving Image reopened earlier this year, with a brand new extension building. We were responsible for the redesign of the identity and all signage/wayfinding. You should visit; the museum's collection is fascinating.

Vitra ID chair campaign **ABOUT:** Campaign for Vitra's new office chair system, motion and print. **DESIGN:** karlssonwilker inc. **ART DIRECTION & DESIGN:** Nicole Jacek and Hjalti Karlsson **DATE:** 2010

KEITH GODARD

WHAT IS THE REASON FOR THE NAME OF YOUR STUDIO?

Originally I was one of many partners working under the name of WORKS.

When my partners left—some left for California, while another one just moved out of New York—WORKS, which was a corporation, disbanded.

HOW LONG HAVE YOU HAD A STUDIO?

I continued working, changing the name to STUDIOWORKS and becoming the sole proprietor in 1988.

HOW MANY EMPLOYEES (FULL-TIME AND FREELANCE)?

Two, with interns.

HOW MANY PRINCIPALS AND EMPLOYEES ARE DESIGNERS?

One.

DO YOU HAVE A STRATEGIST OR ACCOUNT PERSON ON STAFF?

No, just a bookkeeper part-time.

DESCRIBE YOUR CLIENTELE.

Mostly museums, universities, civic government organizations, and United Nations organizations.

ARE YOU ATTEMPTING TO BROADEN YOUR CLIENT BASE?

No—well, I have some electronic publishing proposals that are a bit of a secret.

DO YOU SPECIALIZE? OR GENERALIZE?

I try to be a Renaissance person of the moment. I suppose that's generalizing.

ARE YOU PRIMARILY PRINT OR VIRTUAL, OR BOTH?

I come out of print, but in recent years I've adapted print ideas to exhibitions, environmental design, and public art.

WHAT PROMPTED YOU TO START A STUDIO?

I could not stand being employed and having a boss.

HOW DID YOU DETERMINE WHERE YOUR STUDIO WOULD BE LOCATED?

After starting in this country in New Haven and then getting my first job at *Fortune* magazine (where I stayed for only three months), my girlfriend found an apartment in the Chelsea Hotel in 1967.

Two architect partners I met at Yale had inherited James Stirling's small office in Union Square and asked me to join them. Little did I know when they asked me that Andy Warhol had his factory two floors below and Saul Steinberg rented a studio on the top floor.

DESCRIBE YOUR AESTHETIC, STYLISTIC (EVEN PHILOSOPHIC) APPROACH TO DESIGN.

That might need a whole chapter in itself, but in a nutshell, being British somehow set the childhood tone. I was brought up with the comfortable, literal way of drawing visual things and later discovered surrealism when I went to college.

I never became interested in following any style after the British approach, as it seemed rather archaic to me.

Keith Godard reviews Q.R. code patterns in his studio on Vesey Street with Ho-ling Fong, design assistant.

Poster commissioned by the Adirondack Film Society for the 2004 Lake Placid Film Festival **ABOUT:** The image is a composite of some of the species of fish in the lake. **SIZE:** 37 in. x 27 in. **MEDIUM:** Offset lithography

I suppose eventually I believed in modernism, but I never start by searching for an idea that would be of a decorated essence or a way of doing things in the moment like "being in." Somehow, solutions develop intuitively, so that ideas emerge from the struggle to arrive at an appropriate solution with some spirit embedded in them. And if it has the spicing of poetry and an ingredient of humor, it makes me smile, and I hope does so for others.

HOW MUCH FREEDOM DO YOU ALLOW INDIVIDUAL DESIGNERS?

My budgets often allow no time for hours of free experiment. Mostly my designers have been students of mine, so they come with a fascination with how I go about things. I let them in on all my solutions to problems, some of which are ridiculous, some corny, some the mark of occasional brilliance. If the designer is in agreement as to a compatible direction, then I let them make variations on a theme or concept within guidelines and parameters.

HOW WOULD YOU DEFINE COLLABORATION AS PRACTICED IN YOUR STUDIO?

The question above sort of explains this.

COULD YOUR STUDIO GET ALONG WITHOUT YOU FOR ANY PERIOD OF TIME?

That is a real problem, as I have a small studio and projects in France, and I am away generally six weeks in the year, but I have found that, being up to electronic communications snuff, I can keep up with supply and demand in New York. I guess eventually one will not need a studio in a big metropolis and be able to work anywhere.

DO YOU HAVE A LONG-TERM PLAN FOR SUSTAINABILITY OR GROWTH?

At my age and time of working, and the general feeling I am part of the 99 percent, just to get enough commissions would be greatly appreciated.

WHAT IS THE MOST CHALLENGING PART OF HAVING A STUDIO?

Dealing not so much with the creative output but the daily nitty-gritty of cashflow, putting out fires with clients and helpers, and deciding what to do next year when the lease is up.

DESCRIBE THE MOST SATISFYING PROJECT(S) OF THE PAST YEAR.

Commission for another mural after a client saw Twenty-Third Street station on the R/N train. Reprinting of our Empire State Building "Guide to the Views" in seven foreign languages, being invited to submit a proposal for the Tubman-Garrett Riverfront Park sculpture in Wilmington on the subject of the underground liberation of slavery, and the exhibition of work at the Four Zero Art Space in Hangzhou, China, titiled "Unfolding Keith Godard."

(TOP) Poster for Keith Godard's history of graphic design lecture series, organized by AIGA **MEDIUM:** Offset lithography **SIZE:** 38 in. x 24 in. **(BOTTOM)** *Memories of Twenty-Third Street* **ABOUT:** Mosaic mural for Twenty-Third Street subway station. The hats represent people who either lived or traversed Twenty-Third Street between 1880 and 1920. Passengers can "wear" the hats by standing beneath them while waiting for the train. **CLIENT:** New York City Metropolitan Arts for Transit **DATE:** 2005

KIND COMPANY

WHAT IS THE REASON FOR THE NAME OF YOUR STUDIO?
We liked the sound of it and wanted something a bit out of the ordinary. The two words sound nice together and it's served us well, even in all its different iterations: Kind and Company, The Kind Company, KindCo, KCO, and so on.

HOW LONG HAVE YOU HAD A STUDIO?
We've been in business since 2004.

HOW MANY EMPLOYEES (FULL-TIME AND FREELANCE)?
We are two full-time partners. Occasionally, on a project-by-project basis, we collaborate with individuals.

HOW MANY PRINCIPALS AND EMPLOYEES ARE DESIGNERS?
We are both designers and partners in the business.

OTHERS?
No.

DO YOU HAVE A STRATEGIST OR ACCOUNT PERSON ON STAFF?
No, since we are a company of two, we share all tasks—including design, account management, business development, answering the phone, taking out the trash, making coffee, shipping, etc. Each partner carries their own weight.

DESCRIBE YOUR CLIENTELE.
Our clientele is made up of small- to medium-sized businesses—art galleries, restaurants, architects, authors, bookstores, and archives. We've been very fortunate to find entrepre-

neurial clients who are interested in using design as a tool to help communicate their ideas, products, and services.

ARE YOU ATTEMPTING TO BROADEN YOUR CLIENT BASE?
Yes, we're always open to broadening our client base but more interested in taking on projects with like-minded people. Our types of clients change from project to project. We're always learning new and exciting things about our clients' businesses and enjoy the variety.

DO YOU SPECIALIZE? OR GENERALIZE?
We generalize in the sense that we design in many areas—a single logo to a more comprehensive identity system, printed collateral, and websites, both simple in nature and more robust content management systems.

ARE YOU PRIMARILY PRINT OR VIRTUAL, OR BOTH?
Our projects have been about even—fifty-fifty, print and web.

WHAT PROMPTED YOU TO START A STUDIO?
We both had experiences working for larger companies and were never truly satisfied. We wanted to design directly for people like us—small businesses, entrepreneurs, clients who share our interests and value design. Opening our own, independent graphic design studio was the logical next step for us.

PRINCIPALS
GREG D'ONOFRIO
PATRICIA BELEN

FOUNDED
2004

LOCATION
NEW YORK, NY

EMPLOYEES
2 FULL-TIME
PARTNERS

Kind Company partners Patricia Belen and Greg D'Onofrio

HOW DID YOU DETERMINE WHERE YOUR STUDIO WOULD BE LOCATED?

Our studio started in our New York apartment, then moved to a window-less basement office space, then to a larger storefront space, then back to our apartment, where it currently resides and feels most comfortable. Ultimately, we decided a big studio office was not right for us. Like running a small business, finding the "right" location has always been a work in progress.

DESCRIBE YOUR AESTHETIC, STYLISTIC (EVEN PHILOSOPHIC) APPROACH TO DESIGN.

Our work embodies the belief that good graphic design is simple, smart, and usable. Design is successful when it speaks in an honest and direct way. Our approach has always been centered around our clients' communication problems and business goals. So, the solutions we recommend are always tailored, but still emphasize our beliefs as to what constitutes good design—a combination of function and aesthetics.

HOW MUCH FREEDOM DO YOU ALLOW INDIVIDUAL DESIGNERS?

Since we ourselves are the designers, you could say we have all the freedom in the world. However, we work better when a project has criteria based on specific client goals. Limitations, whether from the client or self-imposed, help us think and design smarter.

(TOP) Wolfsonian–FIU "Thoughts on Democracy" exhibition poster **DATE:** 2011 (BOTTOM) John McWhinnie Gallery printed collateral **DATE:** 2011

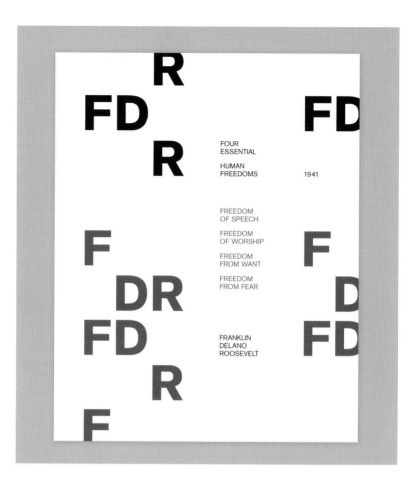

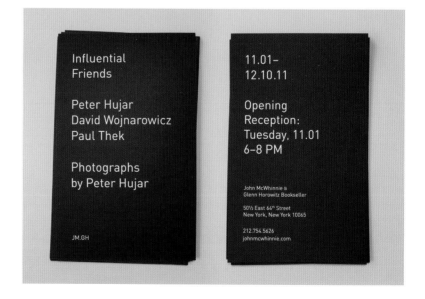

HOW WOULD YOU DEFINE COLLABORATION AS PRACTICED IN YOUR STUDIO?

After eight years in business, we've learned to collaborate on virtually all aspects of the design studio. Design is a collaborative process—between the two partners and also between the studio and client. But we also work together on proposals, client meetings, phone calls, ideas for new projects, etc. There is hardly a task one of us does independently, without the other partner's guidance.

COULD YOUR STUDIO GET ALONG WITHOUT YOU FOR ANY PERIOD OF TIME?

Not likely. Fortunately, we've never had the situation where one of us could not be involved in the studio at any given time. Since we're partners in both business and life, it's all integrated. If we decide to take a vacation, the studio is also on vacation, which hasn't been a problem thus far.

DO YOU HAVE A LONG-TERM PLAN FOR SUSTAINABILITY OR GROWTH?

We definitely want to keep our studio small, so we have no plans to grow in that area. Honestly, we do not have plans for sustainability. As long as we continue to focus on projects that interest us, there will always be more work to do. We're optimistic!

WHAT IS THE MOST CHALLENGING PART OF HAVING A STUDIO?

Time management is a challenge for a two-person studio. We have to balance the time spent doing the actual work, securing new clients, managing the day-to-day business, and working on our ongoing design history projects (see next question).

DESCRIBE THE MOST SATISFYING PROJECT(S) OF THE PAST YEAR.

For the past few years, we've devoted a great deal of time to Display (http://www.thisisdisplay.org), our curated collection of modern, mid-twentieth-century graphic design. It's become our mission to document and write about these important books, periodicals, advertisements, and ephemera. We hope Display educates others about the work of lesser-known designers and the lesser-known work of well-known design pioneers. It's been incredibly satisfying to know others share the same interests and use Display as a resource for graphic design history. Ultimately, we look forward to this project becoming a stepping stone for us to author and self-publish our own materials.

(TOP) Mark Dixon Architect identity and print collateral DATE: 2011 (BOTTOM) Castle Members Club identity and print collateral DATE: 2011

LANDERS MILLER DESIGN

WHAT IS THE REASON FOR THE NAME OF YOUR STUDIO?
Before we officially/legally had a studio, we were both doing a good amount of independent freelance work. Our clients knew we were married and often wrote checks for payment out to "Landers Miller," so to keep things simple, when we officially started our studio as a legal entity, we just stuck with the idea of using our last names.

HOW LONG HAVE YOU HAD A STUDIO?
Five years, officially.

HOW MANY EMPLOYEES (FULL-TIME AND FREELANCE)?
It's just the two of us full-time; we bring freelancers on when we need them—basically scale according to need.

HOW MANY PRINCIPALS AND EMPLOYEES ARE DESIGNERS?
We are both designers and both have a background in graphic design. Colleen has shifted her focus more to interaction design.

DO YOU HAVE A STRATEGIST OR ACCOUNT PERSON ON STAFF?
No. We often talk to others who are in the same position as us or who have been in our position, who can share ideas and methods that they have used, to plan and evolve our business.

DESCRIBE YOUR CLIENTELE.
We really work with a pretty broad range of clients and businesses, which vary in both their market and scale. We do quite a bit of work with small or independent start-ups, and our steady base of work really comes from educational institutions and publishing companies.

ARE YOU ATTEMPTING TO BROADEN YOUR CLIENT BASE?
Yes, but we are planning on doing this as a more focused exercise. We want to target businesses in specific markets. We really love working with clients in the food industry, and we're going to try to get involved in the pet market as well.

DO YOU SPECIALIZE? OR GENERALIZE?
We generalize, though there are certain areas of design that we simply do not have experience in, which makes it difficult to break into those markets. That can be both a blessing and a bit frustrating. On one hand you get to be really well versed in your areas of practice; on the other hand, we love the idea of trying new things and really getting to explore other areas of practice in design.

ARE YOU PRIMARILY PRINT OR VIRTUAL, OR BOTH?
Both.

WHAT PROMPTED YOU TO START A STUDIO?
Colleen was working as a full-time designer at a small studio and I was freelancing full-time with various agencies, but we were also both doing a lot of independent freelance projects. Ultimately we had enough independent freelance work to really keep us both more than busy. We decided to go for it and leave our full-time positions working for others and try working for ourselves.

PRINCIPALS
COLLEEN MILLER
RICK LANDERS

FOUNDED
2006

LOCATION
NEW YORK

EMPLOYEES
2 FULL-TIME +
FREELANCERS

HOW DID YOU DETERMINE WHERE YOUR STUDIO WOULD BE LOCATED?

When we started, we were working out of our second room in our 600-square-foot apartment in Brooklyn. It was a big enough risk to drop our steady, reliable, full-time jobs, so it was a matter of necessity to keep our expenses low and play it safe by using the space we had available to us. Eventually, after a little more than a year, we had a solid, steady client base and income; we were able to go out and rent a space, in Manhattan. We paired up with a couple of other independent designers and were able to rent a larger space, giving us the added bonus of other folks to talk to and even collaborate with from time to time on projects.

DESCRIBE YOUR AESTHETIC, STYLISTIC (EVEN PHILOSOPHIC) APPROACH TO DESIGN.

We don't really have a specific aesthetic; all of our clients are different and therefore the solutions to the assignments need to be specific to their audience. If there is one thing that is consistent with our approach to design, it is that we always try to simplify things as much as we can to make the messaging and presentation clear and direct. Once we have simplified, then aesthetic considerations come into play.

HOW MUCH FREEDOM DO YOU ALLOW INDIVIDUAL DESIGNERS?

When we hire freelancers to work with us it's because we want to bring something to the project that we cannot necessarily do on our own. We always try to bring designers on who have something different to bring to the table or who do something better than we can. We want designers who work with

us to have a sense of ownership of the project and not just to be a set of hands.

HOW WOULD YOU DEFINE COLLABORATION AS PRACTICED IN YOUR STUDIO?

We typically both work on the same projects simultaneously to start and then evolve the work together by working on what the other started or by offering feedback and criticism. When there's an outside designer involved, it's the same; they are just as responsible as we are for putting ideas out. It's a pretty open and organic process; there's never really one specific way that we work. Eventually one of us assumes the role of project lead to finish the assignment, but the other is still equally involved through completion.

COULD YOUR STUDIO GET ALONG WITHOUT YOU FOR ANY PERIOD OF TIME?

That's been the hardest thing to do— to get away and let go. Because we fill the roles of designers and project managers, we deal with the clients directly. When we need to get away or go on vacation or take a break, it's really on us to give our clients a heads up a fair amount of time in advance and just remind them of the timing. Maybe one day we'll be in a position where we have a full-time employee or two who we trust will manage things when we are out.

DO YOU HAVE A LONG-TERM PLAN FOR SUSTAINABILITY OR GROWTH?

We have always wanted to have a small studio and never have really wanted to be in a position where we are more managerial than hands on. It would be nice to have one or maybe two full-time designers to work with, both for the opportunity to give someone else the chance to grow and to see what it's like to operate a

(TOP) *Philadelphia University Graphic Design Blog* **ABOUT:** We wanted to give back to our alma mater. Rather than donating money we donated our design services to the school by providing the graphic design communication program with their own mobile responsive website designed to promote the program, students, and work. The site is built using WordPress as the content management system. **SITE DEVELOPMENT:** GrowthSpark (**BOTTOM LEFT**) Cocomama package design **ABOUT:** is a new food brand focused on providing healthy, all natural and organic foods that are also gluten free. Their first product launch was a ready-to-eat quinoa cereal that is very similar to oatmeal, except made with a very interesting and eclectic group of ingredients. It was this eclectic selection of ingredients that inspired the identity. www.cocomamafoods. com (**BOTTOM RIGHT**) *Stop, Think, Go, Do* **ABOUT:** This book takes a hard look at graphic design that alters behavior through type, color, form, and composition for various purposes and with distinct results, but always with one common purpose: to manipulate the conscious and subconscious. Each of the eight chapters includes an opening typographic illustration meant to support the theme and content of the chapter.

(TOP): Food for Thought **ABOUT:** An iPhone app that addresses widespread misunderstandings about food consumption by providing healthy recommendations and a system for tracking nutrition changes that can consciously effect improvements in personal eating habits. Since designing Food for Thought as her thesis presentation in Interaction Design at the School of Visual Arts, Colleen has partnered with the Food Network to help bring this project to fruition. **DESIGN & CON-CEPT:** Colleen Miller **ILLUSTRATION:** Landers Miller Design **(BOTTOM):** *Marilyn & Me* **ABOUT:** A limited edition, hardcover book that tells the intimate story of Marilyn Monroe before her fall and a young photographer—Lawrence Schiller, on his way to the top. The book includes an original text by Schiller and an extraordinary collection of photographs—over two-thirds of which have never or rarely been published. **BOOK CONCEPT DESIGN:** Landers Miller Design **FINAL BOOK DESIGN:** Taschen

small business, but also for the opportunity for us to maybe be able to take a step back from the day-to-day responsibilities and focus on other areas of growing or changing the business, or just even to explore and experiment with personal projects/ interests more often.

WHAT IS THE MOST CHALLENGING PART OF HAVING A STUDIO?

For a solo or small operation like ours, it's definitely the challenge of juggling and balancing so many responsibilities every day. We're responsible for research, concepting the ideas, executing the design, and following through with actual production, as well as the fact that we manage the clients and all areas of communication: meetings, phone calls, presentations, writing the proposals, figuring out the budgets, dealing with the books—and that's just existing clients. New or potential clients are a whole other range of work that we need to budget time for. It can be stressful, but it's also pretty fulfilling to know that we are often doing the same level of work that a full-time staff of people is doing elsewhere, and we're doing it on our own.

DESCRIBE THE MOST SATISFYING PROJECT(S) OF THE PAST YEAR.

In 2009 Colleen was accepted into the MFA Interaction Design program at the School of Visual Arts. She was part of the inaugural class, which graduated in 2011. As part of her thesis she concepted and developed an app titled "Food for Thought" to provide people with helpful steps to take and reminders about their eating habits. Soon after graduating from SVA, Colleen brought the idea to the Food Network and is currently working with them to produce the app.

New York Times 36 Hours **ABOUT:** This book features 125 itineraries for quick, memorable European trips. The book is a compilation of the popular *Times* 36 Hours series with new photography and custom-designed maps. **ART DIRECTION:** Marco Zivny and Josh Baker **LAYOUT & DESIGN:** Landers Miller **DESIGN ILLUSTRATION:** Olimpia Zagnoli **EDITOR:** Barbara Ireland

LSDSPACE / UN MUNDO FELIZ

WHAT IS THE REASON FOR THE NAME OF YOUR STUDIO?

"LSDspace" is meant to evoke a vision of design as "an altered state of consciousness" through creativity. Our goal is to help our clients reach a different vision of their reality and see communication from a different perspective. "Un Mundo Feliz" is a project based on self-expression and collaboration that focuses on questions of public and social interest. The name comes from the Aldous Huxley book *A Brave New World*, and it suggests a utopian vision of the world in contrast to promises of happiness.

HOW LONG HAVE YOU HAD A STUDIO?

Nine years.

HOW MANY EMPLOYEES (FULL-TIME AND FREELANCE)?

Two full-time designers. However, we do work online. In every project we try to collaborate with other designers, illustrators, photographers, and other design studios such as Lacucharanoexiste, AzulFaro10, or the typographer Manuel Ponce.

HOW MANY PRINCIPALS AND EMPLOYEES ARE DESIGNERS?

We are two designers coming from different backgrounds. Sonia Díaz has studied design, psychology, marketing, and journalism. Gabriel Martínez studied philosophy and design.

OTHERS?

We collaborate regularly with Isabel García, who is trained as an art his-

torian and museum professional, and with Cristina Hernanz, a designer and illustrator who also works on information graphics for the web.

DO YOU HAVE A STRATEGIST OR ACCOUNT PERSON ON STAFF?

No.

DESCRIBE YOUR CLIENTELE.

Our clients are essentially small companies, and we also work for independent projects. We are now working for a small company dedicated to market studies (Market Arena), a family-owned wine company (Tinedo Winery), Designers Association of Madrid (DIMAD), South American Biennale of Design (BID), a system engineering company (IDF), an independent art space (espacio E), a university museum (Veterinary Museum, Complutense University, Madrid), Manuel Estrada Design, and the publishing company Promopress. As activists we collaborate independently with nongovernmental institutions.

ARE YOU ATTEMPTING TO BROADEN YOUR CLIENT BASE?

Not really. Most of our time is dedicated to education. We don't have much time and space to look for new clients. Most of our projects come to the studio through friends, old clients, and acquaintances.

DO YOU SPECIALIZE? OR GENERALIZE?

We work in a small scale that allows us to generalize and adapt to the different needs of our clients. We think that it is difficult to specialize if you work for small companies.

PRINCIPALS
SONIA DÍAZ
GABRIEL MARTÍNEZ

FOUNDED
2003

LOCATION
MADRID, SPAIN

EMPLOYEES
**2 FULL-TIME +
FREELANCERS**

(TOP) BP/Macondo CLIENT: Personal project MEDIUM: Poster DESIGNERS: Sonia Díaz & Gabriel Martínez DATE: 2010 (BOTTOM) Spanish revolution FORMAT: Sticker CLIENT: Personal project supporting the spanish movement #democraciarealya DESIGNERS: Sonia Díaz and Gabriel Martínez DATE: 2011

ARE YOU PRIMARILY PRINT OR VIRTUAL, OR BOTH?

We are graphic communicators primarily. Our work is intended to be printed. However, we also produce designs for digital media and online projects.

WHAT PROMPTED YOU TO START A STUDIO?

The opportunity to combine practical design with education. From the beginning, we realized that it was complicated to combine both activities when working for a big company. Also, having a studio allows a closer relationship with the clients.

HOW DID YOU DETERMINE WHERE YOUR STUDIO WOULD BE LOCATED?

After studying design and art we got settled in Madrid, since it was the Spanish city with the best job opportunities. Time has gone by and we are still here. We like Madrid because is a "collage city," a melting pot where cultural activity and business come together.

DESCRIBE YOUR AESTHETIC, STYLISTIC (EVEN PHILOSOPHIC) APPROACH TO DESIGN.

Design for us is a conceptual issue. We are interested in the discourse, the content. We have always had a didactic view of communication and design. From the graphic activism point of view, in Un Mundo Feliz, we propose a realistic vision that we call "bastard pop design" which involves the use of simple media, images, and tools of low resolution that everybody can use.

HOW MUCH FREEDOM DO YOU ALLOW INDIVIDUAL DESIGNERS?

We are a small studio, which allows us to adapt to any situation very rapidly. We work with flexible schedules, and the working groups can change easily. From the creative point of view, the limitations are bigger since clients are not very knowledgeable about design and the budgets are usually very low.

HOW WOULD YOU DEFINE COLLABORATION AS PRACTICED IN YOUR STUDIO?

We are always open to collaborating with other designers and clients with low budgets. Our working speed is limited, so we like to grab the moment, choose what we like and what interests us, even if it is not very profitable.

COULD YOUR STUDIO GET ALONG WITHOUT YOU FOR ANY PERIOD OF TIME?

No. The studio's output reflects what Sonia and Gabriel are and think. If either of us is not present the project will change radically.

DO YOU HAVE A LONG-TERM PLAN FOR SUSTAINABILITY OR GROWTH?

While we like what we do and how we do it, we don't have any plans to expand. To grow will require effort and money that we don't have. It is hard to be small, but that allows us to administer our time more conveniently.

WHAT IS THE MOST CHALLENGING PART OF HAVING A STUDIO?

We are totally responsible for our success and failures. This stimulates our work.

DESCRIBE THE MOST SATISFYING PROJECT(S) OF THE PAST YEAR.

One was the book *Imagomundi*. After publishing *Pictopia*, the publishing company proposed a project about pictograms from a commercial perspective. The book combines creativity with education. We invited our masters Aaron Marcus and Félix Beltrán to write the introduction texts. The book gathers 1,450 pictograms and pictographic illustrations and also includes a short timeline showing pictos designers from Isotype until now. Another interesting project was curating the exhibition "Where Ideas Are Born: Juggler's Notebooks," which shows works of the designer Manuel Estrada. The purpose of the show is to visualize the working process of the designer through his working notebooks. It is a traveling exhibition that will be on display in Spain, Finland, Germany, and the USA.

Books Bomb **FORMAT:** Poster **CLIENT:** Library-Documentation Centre of MUSAC / Contemporary Art Museum Castilla y León **DESIGNERS:** Sonia Díaz and Gabriel Martínez **DATE:** 2010

MASONBARONET

WHAT IS THE REASON FOR THE NAME OF YOUR STUDIO?

Frances: The name of the studio comes from the last names of the founder (Willie Baronet) and the owner (Holly Mason). The studio was originally founded in 1992 as GibbsBaronet by Steve Gibbs and Willie Baronet. After fourteen years of growth—both in the company and personally—Willie sold the company to his protégé, Holly Mason, in 2006. It's actually pretty interesting in contrast to a lot of the other studios in our area. You saw more founders' and owners' names on the door back in the day, but a lot of the younger studios (and I would still consider us a young agency) have more abstract names. I couldn't imagine us having anything but the name we have.

HOW LONG HAVE YOU HAD A STUDIO?

Frances: The firm will celebrate its twenty-year anniversary in February. Although it has been under the current ownership for just over five years, Holly Mason has been part of the firm since 1998. I joined Mason-Baronet as CD in May 2012.

HOW MANY EMPLOYEES (FULL-TIME AND FREELANCE)?

Frances: We have five full-time employees including myself, three part-time employees, and a pool of about four to five freelancers that we use on a regular basis.

HOW MANY PRINCIPALS AND EMPLOYEES ARE DESIGNERS?

Frances: We have a team of three creatives: Holly is the ECD and president, I am the CD, and we have one full-time AD. The AD and I do all of the concept and design work, along with our freelancers.

OTHERS?

Frances: We have two account managers, an office manager, a strategist, and an accountant.

DO YOU HAVE A STRATEGIST OR ACCOUNT PERSON ON STAFF?

Frances: Yes.

DESCRIBE YOUR CLIENTELE.

Holly: Our clientele consists of game changers in the professional service, hospitality, technology, and healthcare sectors who understand how strong strategy and smart design can help them to stand out and outsmart—not outspend—their competition.

ARE YOU ATTEMPTING TO BROADEN YOUR CLIENT BASE?

Holly: Yes, we're always looking for new clients who are a good fit. We've recently completed some work for more luxury, lifestyle brands and are looking to grow that sector in particular.

DO YOU SPECIALIZE? OR GENERALIZE?

Holly: Our specialty is integrated marketing and helping game-changers to distill their complex messages. We've been particularly successful in sectors that have traditionally been more conservative and risk-averse when it comes to their marketing—such as law firms, financial businesses, and healthcare providers. We've helped their brands to stand out with unique, hard-hitting, as well as sensory creative.

ARE YOU PRIMARILY PRINT OR VIRTUAL, OR BOTH?

Holly: Both. We help our clients to ensure brand consistency (visually and experientially) across all touch points with their clients and potential clients—regardless of the media.

WHAT PROMPTED YOU TO START A STUDIO?

Holly: I had been working with Willie Baronet for nearly a decade. I believed strongly in the culture, philosophies, and work of the firm. When I saw Willie begin to pursue other interests, I wanted to see the agency continue to grow and thrive, so I approached him about taking over the firm. I acquired the agency in 2006.

HOW DID YOU DETERMINE WHERE YOUR STUDIO WOULD BE LOCATED?

Holly: Interestingly, at the same time I was acquiring the firm, we were being bought out of our lease by the House of Blues. We wanted to find something that was more unique than your traditional high-rise office, and convenience and safety were key as well. Something open and conducive to the collaboration of our business—with lots of natural light. We were fortunate to find office space in a historic building located downtown, in

PRINCIPALS
**HOLLY MASON,
EXECUTIVE CREATIVE
DIRECTOR**

**FRANCES YLLANA,
CREATIVE DIRECTOR**

FOUNDED
1992

LOCATION
DALLAS, TX

EMPLOYEES
**5 FULL-TIME,
3 PART-TIME,
+ FREELANCERS**

(TOP) Inside MasonBaronet, design library **(BOTTOM LEFT)** Creative director Frances Yllana and executive creative director, president, and owner Holly Mason

Heads Up Technologies user interface design

the Landmark Center. We have large concrete columns, high ceilings, concrete floors, and exposed brick walls. Kind of industrial but finished out to integrate with the sophistication and simplicity of our brand.

DESCRIBE YOUR AESTHETIC, STYLISTIC (EVEN PHILOSOPHIC) APPROACH TO DESIGN.

Frances: I come from a Communication Design program that put a huge emphasis on concept rather than just design. The first place I worked right out of school was exactly the same way. Every creative critique started with traditional pencils, and you had to explain to the CD and the AE how these sketches answered the client's objectives. The best and most solid concepts were then executed—designed and flushed out around the concept. So my philosophy has always been "concept is king, and let it dictate the style/design." Without it, something that is beautifully designed is just that. It doesn't have the same potential to linger in the audience's memory. I worked at that first studio for close to seven years, and since I left there, found that not all studios are as rigorous about making sure there's solid thought behind the pretty pictures. And that's why I loved joining the MasonBaronet team. The studio puts concept in high regard, and Holly has impeccable design taste. We're noted for having a very stylish aesthetic. But the best thing is that the style is backed by solid concept, thought, and strategy. So everything we produce is super polished, but also incredibly smart.

HOW MUCH FREEDOM DO YOU ALLOW INDIVIDUAL DESIGNERS?

Frances: I've been on the team for seven months now, and I think I've al-lowed the designers a lot of freedom in their design and concepting. Most of the work our creative team does is almost 100 percent for the designer to own. We each come up with tons of concepts for each project, so it's more like we're narrowing down what we come up with to our best ideas, and that's what we present to the client and produce. Holly makes sure those ideas are on target. My role is to guide them to make their decisions stronger. Find the details that may have been missed. Give advice as to what might make it better. Fight the battles to make what they want to do work. I believe you have to trust in the decisions you made hiring someone, and it's your place to nurture their growth, and you can't do that by stifling their creativity.

HOW WOULD YOU DEFINE COLLABORATION AS PRACTICED IN YOUR STUDIO?

Frances: Something that surprises me almost every day is how everyone here seems to have a sense of ownership and commitment to the success and growth of the studio. So there's a sense of collaboration on every project. When our team meets other teams from other agencies and studios, I will call our account managers "creatives"—because they are, and they've always been able to add some keen insight into every project. And as it goes for the creative team's collaboration, it happens at every stage of the project. We concept on ideas together. On smaller jobs one creative will manage the entire project and see it through, but on bigger projects, ownership is shared. At the end of the day, it's MasonBaronet's work, and we each do what we can to make it worthy of our reputation.

We also have a great sense of collaboration in the fun we encourage in the studio. Since before I joined the team, MB has had a monthly "Green Bag Lunch" and a "Creative Jam." For each Green Bag Lunch, one of us will put together a presentation to teach the rest of the team something they are more knowledgeable about. And the Creative Jam is when we quit work early one day each month and do something creative together. Like making dioramas of our favorite songs or our State Fair of Texas photo scavenger hunt. We've recently introduced having "Dress-Up Fridays," which are just an opportunity to let go and have fun while we work. I'm odd in the sense that I really enjoy implementing themes, and the team has responded well enough to humor me by playing along. We've had "Slumber Party Friday," where everyone dressed up in our pajamas, "Rock and Roll Friday," "Country Club Friday," and, I think everyone's favorite, "Bro Day," where everyone—including the account manager—dressed up as "dudes." Sometimes it's pretty. Sometimes it's not. But all of it really does contribute to how well we work together.

COULD YOUR STUDIO GET ALONG WITHOUT YOU FOR ANY PERIOD OF TIME?

Holly: Absolutely. We have a great team of entrepreneurial-minded employees who genuinely care about our clients, the work we're producing, and each other. Everyone works hard to ensure we look forward to coming to work every day and that our clients are our biggest fans. I find comfort in knowing I don't have to always be in the office overseeing everything—that the team is taking good care of our culture and our clients.

DO YOU HAVE A LONG-TERM PLAN FOR SUSTAINABILITY OR GROWTH?

Holly: Yes, our firm has a marketing and new business plan that helps ensure we're being intentional and proactive in our growth. We meet regularly as a firm to monitor progress and adapt the plan as needed.

Frances: The regular meeting Holly is talking about is a monthly studio-wide strategy session, and it is actually another one of those studio concepts that surprises me. At some of the other studios where I've worked, in regard to the long-term agency strategy, the input of the team members who aren't in a management role has never really been taken into consideration. But here we ask for it on a regular basis. New ideas for marketing ourselves. Sharing new techniques we've researched. Thoughts on how to engage our clients more. I think that adds an incredible amount to the sense of ownership and dedication everyone here has.

WHAT IS THE MOST CHALLENGING PART OF HAVING A STUDIO?

Holly: I think the most challenging part is finding the inner strength and confidence every day you come in to the office to allow you to adapt to new ideas and changes, to have the ability to find the positive in even the most difficult/challenging situations. In the short five years I've owned the firm, we changed offices twice, we were faced with losing someone who was key to our management team after they sustained a life-altering brain injury, we had an employee who serves in the U.S. Army deployed twice to Iraq, and on top of that, we've had to look for ways to restructure and reinvent ourselves during one of the most difficult economic times of our lives. I've learned first hand, time and

again, how things can change so quickly. As a result, I try to focus and keep my team focused on those things in our control and hope it all works out for the best!

DESCRIBE THE MOST SATISFYING PROJECT(S) OF THE PAST YEAR.

Holly: We had an opportunity to work on a very unique project this past year. We were engaged by an engineering firm to partner with them on developing a cabin management system for the aviation industry. We were responsible for designing the user interface of the system and helping to ensure an intuitive and smart user experience. The cabin management system features touch screens that are customized to blend seamlessly into the cabin interior. The system is the first of its kind in that the OEM can customize the design to support their brand and cabin interiors and is scalable to work across their entire product line. The system was just launched at the National Business Aviation Association show in Vegas in October and is standard in Cessna's Citation Ten and optional in their new Cessna Citation M2 via a wireless app user interface that can be accessed through smartphones and tablets.

Frances: I would agree with Holly on that project. But I think a lot of the projects we started at the beginning of the summer have been pretty satisfying to work on. Especially since they encompassed the entire brand—from strategy direction to identity to website and collateral, it's been exciting to see how we've turned some of these companies' brand identities, as well as how they talk about themselves, around so quickly—and so well. Especially since we're closing some of those jobs and seeing how positively our clients, and their clients and referral sources, have responded.

Cirqa Wallcovering advertising campaign

Watercolour

MGMT. DESIGN

WHAT IS THE REASON FOR THE NAME OF YOUR STUDIO?

The studio name was a reaction to the frustrations of being managed by others. And, to be clear, our name predated the band.

HOW LONG HAVE YOU HAD A STUDIO?

Since 2002.

HOW MANY EMPLOYEES (FULL-TIME AND FREELANCE)?

Three full-time, one intern.

HOW MANY PRINCIPALS AND EMPLOYEES ARE DESIGNERS?

All 100 percent.

DO YOU HAVE A STRATEGIST OR ACCOUNT PERSON ON STAFF?

Nope.

DESCRIBE YOUR CLIENTELE.

Clients range from exhibition design for nonprofit arts organizations, art and architecture publications, infographics for online and print, to branding projects and texbook design.

ARE YOU ATTEMPTING TO BROADEN YOUR CLIENT BASE?

We tend to take on projects with content that interests us as designers; we are less inclined to explicitly build a client base. Happily, that unintentional strategy has resulted in a list of clients we like and admire.

DO YOU SPECIALIZE? OR GENERALIZE?

We like to say we specialize in tackling complex bodies of data regardless of subject or medium; so maybe we specialize in a general way.

ARE YOU PRIMARILY PRINT OR VIRTUAL, OR BOTH?

Both, but primarily print.

WHAT PROMPTED YOU TO START A STUDIO?

One of the partners was working freelance and needed help. After that collaboration and realizing how hard we were all working for other people, MGMT. design was formed. We had no business plan, design mandate, or clients; only the common desire to do our own work as a collaborative team.

HOW DID YOU DETERMINE WHERE YOUR STUDIO WOULD BE LOCATED?

Originally we rented desks in a shared office space on the Lower East Side.

We moved to Brooklyn when it became clear that looking at full-size proofs on someone else's desk was inconvenient. We needed more space.

DESCRIBE YOUR AESTHETIC, STYLISTIC (EVEN PHILOSOPHIC) APPROACH TO DESIGN.

Our prevailing approach is to place investigation and process ahead of a single design aesthetic. All projects begin with extensive research and maintain a high level of conceptual and visual rigor throughout the process.

PRINCIPALS
ALICIA CHENG
SARAH GEPHART

FOUNDED
2002

LOCATION
BROOKLYN, NY

EMPLOYEES
3 FULL-TIME

(TOP) Sarah Gephart (left), Alicia Cheng (right) PHOTO: Harry Zernike

We try to create intelligent design solutions that visually enrich and clearly communicate the content; each project is viewed as an opportunity to learn, explore new ideas, and experiment with materials and production techniques.

HOW MUCH FREEDOM DO YOU ALLOW INDIVIDUAL DESIGNERS?

Each designer comes to MGMT. based on the strength of their own individual design talents as well as their fit within the studio; we encourage each designer to express their own aesthetic within the project parameters. Having two art directors/partners also keeps the project within the MGMT. ethos.

HOW WOULD YOU DEFINE COLLABORATION AS PRACTICED IN YOUR STUDIO?

In the office there is a spirit of open collaboration that we promote and encourage. It works because everyone can contribute their individual interpretation without being territorial. It makes a stronger product in the end. Plus it's more fun.

COULD YOUR STUDIO GET ALONG WITHOUT YOU FOR ANY PERIOD OF TIME?

The studio has operated fairly independently when both partners were traveling. We are very hands-on so it's hard to stay away for too long.

Luckily we have had fantastic people working for us, which makes everything easier.

DO YOU HAVE A LONG-TERM PLAN FOR SUSTAINABILITY OR GROWTH?

When we first started MGMT. we were focused mainly on staying afloat. As the years went by, we learned what works and what doesn't and what studio scale is the most comfortable for us. Our long-range plan is: more of the same, but better.

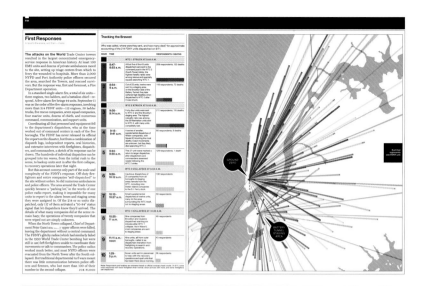

Map for *New York* magazine **ABOUT:** Included in the 9/11 anniversary issue, this infographic shows the ten waves of first responders of the NYFD, NYPD, and EMS immediately following the attacks. Using dispatches throughout the day, the infographic shows who was called, where they were sent, and how many died. **ART DIRECTION:** Alicia Cheng **DESIGN:** Erola Boix

Knoll

A MODERNIST UNIVERSE

Brian Lutz

RIZZOLI
NEW YORK

Knoll: A Modernist Universe **ABOUT:** Intended to be a companion volume to Massimo Vignelli's 1981 book, this publication contains a comprehensive history of the famed furniture design company founded by Hans Knoll. **ART DIRECTION:** Sarah Gephart, Alicia Cheng **DESIGN:** Michael Brenner, Asad Pervaiz **PHOTO:** Harry Zernike

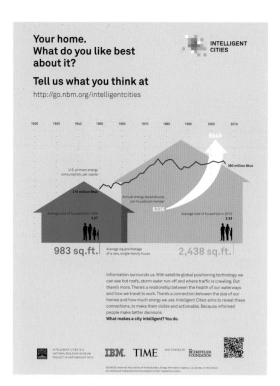

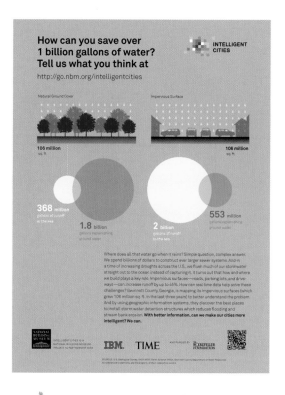

ABOUT: A project that explored the intersection of information technology and urban design. Scope included the project identity and featured a series of six infographic 'mashups' that appeared in *TIME* magazine. **ART DIRECTION:** Sarah Gephart, Alicia Cheng **DESIGN:** Erola Boix

ABOUT: MGMT. has provided ongoing exhibition layout and graphic design services for the International Center of Photography in New York. Typical scope includes the design of the exhibition identities and graphic components as well as all related print materials, advertisements, and brand guidelines. **ART DIRECTION:** Alicia Cheng

WHAT IS THE MOST CHALLENGING PART OF HAVING A STUDIO?

Keeping the workload on an even keel, planning months ahead while still keeping an eye on the ball, trying to balance the bread-and-butter projects while still being able to take on the crazy rushed no-money projects we can't say no to.

DESCRIBE THE MOST SATISFYING PROJECT(S) OF THE PAST YEAR.

We did a project with the National Building Museum that explored the intersection of information technology and urban design. The project involved a series of thought-provoking information graphics that appeared monthly in *TIME* magazine. The ads focused on revealing unexpected connections between independent data sets and were based on a "Powers of Ten" concept, moving from the individual outward to the national level. The project incorporated identity design, information design, a publication, and a potential exhibition. For us, the perfect cross-medium trifecta plus one.

Photo by Marta Bacigalupo

PIETRO CORRAINI

WHAT IS THE REASON FOR THE NAME OF YOUR STUDIO?
Well… it's my name.

HOW LONG HAVE YOU HAD A STUDIO?
Five years.

HOW MANY EMPLOYEES (FULL-TIME AND FREELANCE)?
Two or three freelance.

HOW MANY PRINCIPALS AND EMPLOYEES ARE DESIGNERS?
We are all graphic designers.

OTHERS?
Usually we have an intern for three or four months every year.

DO YOU HAVE A STRATEGIST OR ACCOUNT PERSON ON STAFF?
No.

DESCRIBE YOUR CLIENTELE.
I mostly work with cultural and artistic institutions and societies. In the last few years I have also undertaken many collaborations within the food world. Generally I am interested in projects done by people who love what they do.

ARE YOU ATTEMPTING TO BROADEN YOUR CLIENT BASE?
Every day!

DO YOU SPECIALIZE? OR GENERALIZE?
I apply a specific method and spirit that I use to approach many different fields. Somehow I'm specialized to generalize.

ARE YOU PRIMARILY PRINT OR VIRTUAL, OR BOTH?
I'm both: it depends on what I have to do. Most of the time I use different media; I concentrate more on the idea and on the concept, leaving the technical stuff to my collaborators or to other studios.

WHAT PROMPTED YOU TO START A STUDIO?
I always worked in my parents' publishing house, but little by little I started doing my own little projects; it slowly grew from there.

HOW DID YOU DETERMINE WHERE YOUR STUDIO WOULD BE LOCATED?
The studio is located in the design district of Milan, where the Fuori Salone, one of the most important events for design, is held in April. Here designers from all over the world come to see what is new and what is going to be new in the next years. Because of that, there are many interesting little shops, small and big studios—not just design but also fashion and architecture; in this way the atmosphere is always really stimulating. (And of course it is really close to my apartment.)

DESCRIBE YOUR AESTHETIC, STYLISTIC (EVEN PHILOSOPHIC) APPROACH TO DESIGN.
I try to communicate the spirit of things, with lightness and joy, embracing the content but being careful not to take liberties with my personal style. The idea of "show don't tell" is behind most of of my work. I get rid of everything that is not strictly necessary, so the content can be shown in the best way.

PRINCIPAL
PIETRO CORRAINI

FOUNDED
2007

LOCATION
MILAN, ITALY

EMPLOYEES
3-4

Book design for *A work of Persol* **DESIGN:** Corraini Studio **ILLUSTRATION:** Harriett Russell **DATE:** 2010

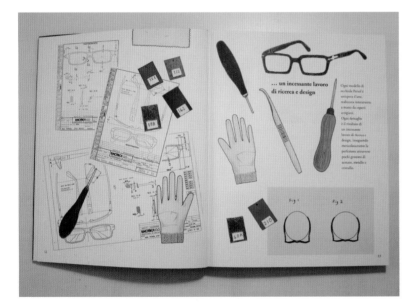

HOW MUCH FREEDOM DO YOU ALLOW INDIVIDUAL DESIGNERS?

In the beginning I want to know them really well, trying to understand their qualities and faults, to understand what are the skills that are more useful for the studio and for my work. Then I want them to know me and my approach to the projects so that we can work together better. With this in mind, I encourage the individual designer to do his/her best, becoming every day more and more independent.

HOW WOULD YOU DEFINE COLLABORATION AS PRACTICED IN YOUR STUDIO?

We often collaborate with other graphic design studios or with authors who come from different fields. This cooperation is really productive to face always-different challenges. With my coworkers the relationship is really informal: We have lunch together at my home (which is really close to the studio), where we cook together. During this break, we have the chance to talk not just about work but also about our personal lives. I think this is a really important moment of the day, because you can resolve the mental stress of the day and better understand the needs of the people who work with you, making for a pleasant work environment.

COULD YOUR STUDIO GET ALONG WITHOUT YOU FOR ANY PERIOD OF TIME?

Yes.

DO YOU HAVE A LONG-TERM PLAN FOR SUSTAINABILITY OR GROWTH?

In the next few months, I'm going to become a father!

WHAT IS THE MOST CHALLENGING PART OF HAVING A STUDIO?

The most challenging part is dealing with new projects, which always present unexpected problems; the best part is finding new solutions for them!

Moviemov **ABOUT:** Identity for a traveling film festival. Made with Mariachiara Zacchi **DATE:** 2011

MOVIEMOV

ITALIAN CINEMA NOW

LA DOPPIA ORA

The double hour

DESCRIBE THE MOST SATISFYING PROJECT(S) OF THE PAST YEAR.

I'm the creative director of *Un Sedicesimo*, a magazine where every issue is made by a different designer who is free to do whatever he or she wants.

Every issue is a different challenge, and every two months I have to work with the printer and the designer to do good work that suits the author's idea, my personal view, and printing and budget realities. It is like being in a different designer's mind every month. For the Leonardo Sonnoli issue, for example, in order to complete the work, we had to put wooden pieces in the printing machine; with Atelier Vostok we drew directly on the film. Every time it is a new process, a completely different workflow for me.

Even with the other projects, such as books, interior design, or large-scale installations, the most exiting part is when I have to do something I've never done before; that's the best way to learn new things!

PLURAL

WHAT IS THE REASON FOR THE NAME OF YOUR STUDIO?

"Plural" stands for everything more than one. More ideas, more collaboration, more experiments, more practice.

HOW LONG HAVE YOU HAD A STUDIO?

Plural has been a studio practice since July, 2008.

HOW MANY EMPLOYEES (FULL-TIME AND FREELANCE)?

Plural currently has one freelance employee and one intern plus the two principals for a total of four heads.

HOW MANY PRINCIPALS AND EMPLOYEES ARE DESIGNERS?

Everyone at Plural is a designer. Renata Graw and Jeremiah Chiu are principals/founders.

OTHERS?

Plural has an extended family of talented web/interactive developers who come aboard when necessary.

DO YOU HAVE A STRATEGIST OR ACCOUNT PERSON ON STAFF?

No; however we do consider ourselves strategic thinkers.

DESCRIBE YOUR CLIENTELE.

We are still developing a solid client base; however, we have been fortunate to work with a great variety of cultural and educational institutions, as well as artists, musicians, and other designers.

PRINCIPALS
**JEREMIAH CHIU
RENATA GRAW**

FOUNDED
2008

LOCATION
CHICAGO, IL

EMPLOYEES
4

ARE YOU ATTEMPTING TO BROADEN YOUR CLIENT BASE?

We are always interested in pursuing new projects with new clients that we believe in. It is within new collaborations—the moment that we are in new territory and uncomfortable—that we learn/discover the most. We are constantly pursuing new interests and experimenting with new ideas within our own personal projects; more often than not, these projects or ideas find their way into our clients' work.

DO YOU SPECIALIZE? OR GENERALIZE?

That is an interesting question. It depends on one's point of view. We specialize in graphic design, but we "generalize" in terms of what that encompasses. We tend to focus on our approach.

ARE YOU PRIMARILY PRINT OR VIRTUAL, OR BOTH?

We are trained primarily as print designers; however, we come from different backgrounds and bring those into the studio. Renata has a background in industrial design. Jeremiah has a background in music. With the increased demand for web/Internet visibility, almost all of our client-initiated print projects eventually enter the digital realm. Right now we work within a variety of contexts, from print to motion/interactive to web. Recently, we created several site-specific interactive installations for gallery exhibitions that are not web-based, but experience-based.

WHAT PROMPTED YOU TO START A STUDIO?

We decided to start the studio while we were nearing the end of graduate school. Neither one of us was interested in working for an agency at the time, and we were both interested in continuing to have conversations about process, theory, and the crea-

Plural studio

tive practice. We were also intrigued by the idea that some of the most innovative and interesting work we were seeing was coming from small studios. We had very little to lose and we were both used to living on a student's budget, so we thought why not continue just a little longer.

With two weeks until the end of the program, we utilized all of the resources available to print and shoot our work and create business cards and a website. At our graduation, when a professor would ask, "So, what are you doing next?" we handed them a business card and asked them to send any referrals our way, which subsequently led to our first real client.

HOW DID YOU DETERMINE WHERE YOUR STUDIO WOULD BE LOCATED?

As we did not have enough money coming in to rent any space, we began working in Renata's lovely basement. After a year, we moved the office to a loft space that is much better suited for our daily practice.

DESCRIBE YOUR AESTHETIC, STYLISTIC (EVEN PHILOSOPHIC) APPROACH TO DESIGN.

We are involved in a conceptually focused practice, one that allows us to evolve the simplest ideas into meaningful solutions through a process of research, exploration, and experimentation. We try not to think about "style"; however, we do naturally have tendencies toward certain elements (typefaces/imagery, etc.).

HOW MUCH FREEDOM DO YOU ALLOW INDIVIDUAL DESIGNERS?

Total freedom. We work collaboratively, especially at the beginning of any project. There are no bad ideas; in fact, we are always pushing for the wildest/weirdest ideas, just to keep things interesting.

Balloonalisa **ABOUT:** 483 Balloons pinned to a grid creating a pixel image of the Mona Lisa. Part of the "We Are Family" exhibition at The Post Family, Chicago. **DATE:** May, 2010.

Mas Context Analog Conference, poster and exhibition installation **CLIENT:** Mas Context Analog Conference

HOW WOULD YOU DEFINE COLLABORATION AS PRACTICED IN YOUR STUDIO?

All of our projects are collaboratively created. We have been working together for some time now, so we are very comfortable working with each other.

Sometimes collaboration means taking each other's files, sometimes just bouncing ideas off each other. Other times it means disagreeing or questioning one another. What I love the most is that I will leave a file with Renata, and when I return the next day, it has always changed in a way that I would not have done myself, but it totally blows me away.

COULD YOUR STUDIO GET ALONG WITHOUT YOU FOR ANY PERIOD OF TIME?

Yes, for sure. Actually, both of us do quite a bit of traveling—we do work a little bit on the road, so we have had some good experience with working remotely. I believe it was during the second year of being open, I went on a few music tours, one in the States, and one in Europe, each lasting about four to six weeks, while Renata held down the studio. I remember sending files back to her from the dark corner of a Belgian bar at 1:00 AM, as it was the only place with free wi-fi. Obviously, when one of us is out, things get a little bit crazy, but this is also why we started the studio, to allow ourselves the freedom to enjoy vacations and explore new adventures.

DO YOU HAVE A LONG-TERM PLAN FOR SUSTAINABILITY OR GROWTH?

We are at a point at which we are having more discussions about the direction of the practice, developing more specific goals. This became very apparent after revising our studio bio. Our original goal was to create design with strong typography and a strong conceptual approach. Now, we realize that both of those attributes are inherently part of everything we do. So our focus now is to create meaningful projects with people that we believe in and support. Our clients are generally very happy with the work we produce, as we are always very transparent about our approach, informing them of our process, and learning from theirs. I would say the long-term plan is to continue to build these meaningful relationships.

WHAT IS THE MOST CHALLENGING PART OF HAVING A STUDIO?

Besides the day-to-day challenges that come with owning your own business, the most challenging part is trying to run a practice where we do not compromise our beliefs in any of the projects that we take on. We must keep ourselves self-motivated and always strive to push ourselves past our comfort zone to create new work and pursue new ideas. These challenges are also the best part of having a studio.

VISUAL ARTS LANDING IN CHICAGO OCT 21 23

Chicago • IL   Geolofts.   mdwfair.org   MDW⟍FAIR
3636 s Iron st

Identity System for MDW-FAIR **ABOUT:** Includes logotype, typeface family, design of all promotional materials, and signage system.

DESCRIBE THE MOST SATISFYING PROJECT(S) OF THE PAST YEAR.

The most satisfying project for us in the past year was actually a summer workshop we attended in Urbino, Italy with Werkplaats Typografie and ISIA Urbino School of Design. Led by Karel Martens, Armand Mevis, Maureen Mooren, and Leonardo Sonnoli, the overarching theme to the workshop was "time." Each participant was encouraged to explore this very open topic as they wished: to define a project and execute it, to evolve a simple idea and discover its form. It was an interesting exercise for both of us, as it gave us the opportunity to experiment and work both individually and collaboratively. Both of our projects resulted in the creation of short videos. Ultimately, having the time to reflect on our practice allowed us a moment to step back, to look at what we had done over the past three years, and to realize how we should move forward.

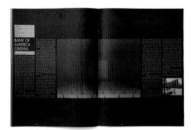

Cover and spreads for *Lumpen Magazine*

(TOP) The Whistler Storefront Installation **ABOUT:** A catalog of the objects found in the space was displayed at full size on the glass, while an interactive projection displayed a spectrum of hues which were determined by the level of sound in the bar (captured with a microphone and custom software developed with Mike Bingaman). **DATE:** 2009 **(BOTTOM)** The Whistler publication **ABOUT:** A self-initiated broadsheet documenting the process for the storefront installation at the Whistler. Sections include initial ideas, proposals, interview, inventory, and statistical information.

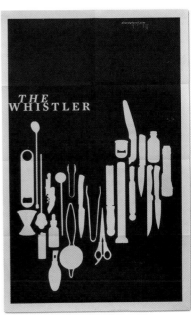

RED

WHAT IS THE REASON FOR THE NAME OF YOUR STUDIO?

SE: We played with a ton of ideas and ended up with the acronym for our names, Rogers Eckersley Design.

SR: It came down to either RED or Tacklebox. I think we made the right decision.

HOW LONG HAVE YOU HAD A STUDIO?

SR: Six years.

HOW MANY EMPLOYEES (FULL-TIME AND FREELANCE)?

SE: Including the two of us, we are a group of five full-time, plus an intern.

HOW MANY PRINCIPALS AND EMPLOYEES ARE DESIGNERS?

SE: Both principals and all staff are trained designers, although we all wear a variety of hats.

OTHERS?

SE: We bring in a bookkeeper every other week, and often collaborate with writers, strategists, photographers, etc. But our staff is 100 percent design.

DO YOU HAVE A STRATEGIST OR ACCOUNT PERSON ON STAFF?

SR: No, we end up being the account people. When it comes to strategy, though, we rely on partnerships.

DESCRIBE YOUR CLIENTELE.

SE: We work with a diverse group of nonprofit, sports, and entertainment clients, who range from huge to tiny to somewhere in the middle.

SR: We try to establish client relationships with people we admire and respect.

ARE YOU ATTEMPTING TO BROADEN YOUR CLIENT BASE?

SE: Quite the opposite. When we partnered up, Stuart and I came from different backgrounds and brought a very unusual mix of clients together. We love that every day is different, but have made a conscious effort to try bringing our areas of focus closer together.

DO YOU SPECIALIZE? OR GENERALIZE?

SR: I think we will consider any interesting project, no matter the industry or medium. We like to try new things. So in that way, you could say we have a strong generalist spirit. In reality, though, there are a few industries that we work in more heavily than others. This really happened organically, but lately we've become more deliberate about marketing ourselves as specialists to those industries.

ARE YOU PRIMARILY PRINT OR VIRTUAL, OR BOTH?

SE: Most of our work is branding, which tends to extend into both areas. That said, we probably think as print designers.

SR: It's becoming really hard to tell the difference. Most of the posters we design for theater, for instance, live a mostly digital life. We rarely go on press anymore.

PRINCIPALS
SAM ECKERSLEY
STUART ROGERS

FOUNDED
2006

LOCATION
NEW YORK, NY

EMPLOYEES
5 FULL-TIME

PHOTOS: José Contreras

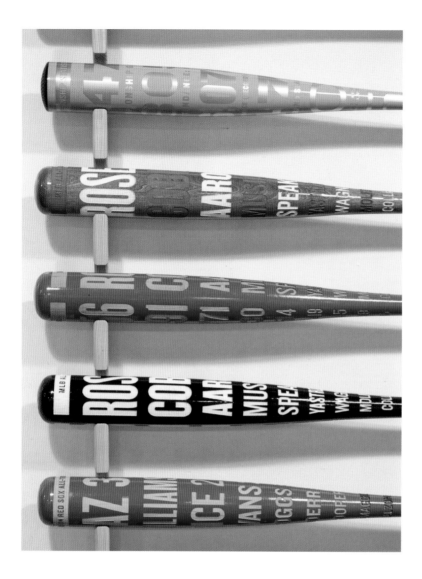

(ABOVE) Stat Bats **CLIENT:** RED **DESIGN:** Stuart Rogers, Sam Eckersley, Eliza Cerdeiros **ENGRAVER:** Laser Magic, Inc.
(ABOVE RIGHT) Super Bowl XLVI **CLIENT:** NFL **CREATIVE DIRECTION** NFL **DESIGN:** Stuart Rogers, Sam Eckersley
(BELOW RIGHT) Canyon of Heroes Campaign **CLIENT:** Alliance for Downtown New York **ART DIRECTION:** Sam Eckersley **DESIGN:** Jane Huschka **PRODUCTION:** Jamus Marquette, Alexandra Marino **PHOTO:** Katharina Stiegler

WHAT PROMPTED YOU TO START A STUDIO?

SE: For me, I think it was the right thing at the right time. I'd finished the masters program at SVA (where I met Stuart), and their motto of "Designer as Author" really planted a seed of wanting to lay my own path. I really enjoy dealing directly with clients and hadn't had an opportunity to do that enough with previous jobs. I was also at a time in my life where starting a studio wasn't a huge risk. We didn't need a large sum of money to open our doors, and if it didn't work after a few months, we could call it quits and look for something full-time.

SR: We had both been to the design MFA program at SVA and had formed valuable relationships with our classmates and faculty, and in the first year or two of the studio almost all of our business somehow tied back to SVA connections (we actually visualized this for a presentation once). So, I think we both sensed that we were plugged in enough to make it work. Also, there is almost no barrier to entry when starting a studio, other than living without a salary for a few months.

HOW DID YOU DETERMINE WHERE YOUR STUDIO WOULD BE LOCATED?

SE: We both lived in Brooklyn, and at the time felt it was important to have a Manhattan address to impress clients. We've gotten over that, but remain in a relatively central part of the city that's close to both clients and home.

SR: Right. It felt like it was somehow less legit to be in Brooklyn—like people would think Sam and I were just sitting around in our sweatpants drawing pictures. That probably seems ridiculous, but it did feel like the Manhattan address made it real at the time. At this point, I think we've become used to it and like being here.

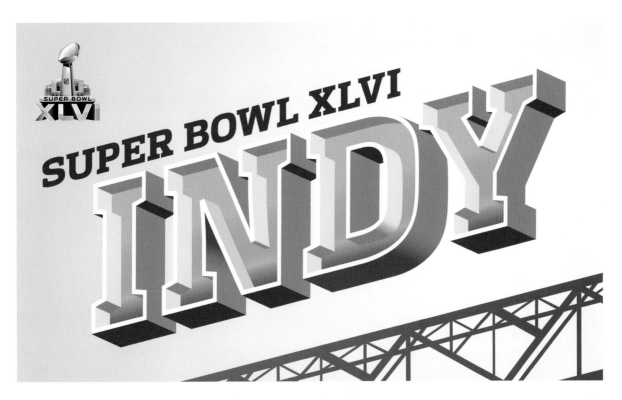

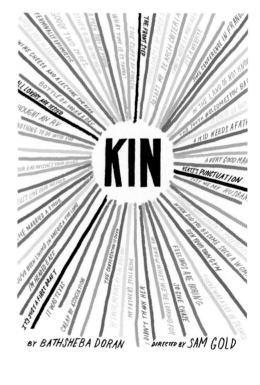

(ABOVE LEFT) Southwest Porch restaurant CLIENT: Southwest Airlines PROJECT LEAD: Civic Entertainment Group ARCHITECTURAL PLAN: Nancy Thiel Architecture DESIGN: Stuart Rogers, Sam Eckersley, Jane Huschka (FAR LEFT) Red Barber Campaign CLIENT: RED DESIGN: Sam Eckersley (LEFT) Kin CLIENT: Playwrights Horizons ART DIRECTION: Stuart Rogers DESIGN & ILLUSTRATION: Jamus Marquette (ABOVE RIGHT) Mimi Awards icon CLIENT: Steinberg Charitable Trust ART DIRECTION: Stuart Rogers DESIGN & ILLUSTRATION: Jane Huschka (BELOW RIGHT) Brooklyn Youth Chorus identity CLIENT: Brooklyn Youth Chorus ART DIRECTION: Stuart Rogers DESIGN: Stuart Rogers, Jane Huschka

DESCRIBE YOUR AESTHETIC, STYLISTIC (EVEN PHILOSOPHIC) APPROACH TO DESIGN.

SE: Everything we do comes with a story and a reason. That's something that Stuart and I really gel on, and work hard with our talented design staff to implement.

SR: Like Sam says, ideas are king. When it comes to execution, we always seem to come back to bold and expressive typography.

HOW MUCH FREEDOM DO YOU ALLOW INDIVIDUAL DESIGNERS?

SR: We offer them a lot of autonomy. Basically, we want to see smart, idea-driven solutions. Beyond that, we allow our designers to explore their own creative styles. We also expect them to interact with our clients.

HOW WOULD YOU DEFINE COLLABORATION AS PRACTICED IN YOUR STUDIO?

SR: When we're working on a project, we will put our research and sketches up on the wall for discussion. Sometimes informal collaboration grows out of that, where someone sees something and shares a thought. Other times, we schedule meetings to discuss the work and everyone's voice is welcome.

COULD YOUR STUDIO GET ALONG WITHOUT YOU FOR ANY PERIOD OF TIME?

SE: Three years ago I would have said no, but because of our balanced partnership and amazing staff I think I could be out of the office for a while without real consequences. Hmmmm.

SR: Yes. I took a two-week vacation this year—my first one of that length since we started the company. We did not go out of business in that time.

DO YOU HAVE A LONG-TERM PLAN FOR SUSTAINABILITY OR GROWTH?

SR: Nothing formal, but we'd be lying if we said this isn't on our minds. A shared goal is to move toward growing industries, and perhaps away from ones that feel like they're on the downslope.

WHAT IS THE MOST CHALLENGING PART OF HAVING A STUDIO?

SE: Being proud of what we create, and making a comfortable living doing it.

SR: The biggest challenge for me is playing so many roles on a daily basis. It's often necessary to transition between taking a client's call, writing a proposal, sketching concepts, and talking numbers. Ultimately, it's rare that we get to put our heads into one task for several hours straight. We consider this something that we want to fix in the future.

DESCRIBE THE MOST SATISFYING PROJECT(S) OF THE PAST YEAR?

SE: Hands down, the most enjoyable project we worked on this year was for Nike. The backstory is that both Stuart and I have always wanted to create products that we could sell… something that was 100 percent ours. Our initial attempt at that was an idea Stuart had, which was to create baseball bats that had stats engraved on them. A few years ago we had created a prototype which Nike saw and loved. This past summer they asked if we could create a line of bats for their store at the College World Series. We got to work with a dream client, produce our own idea, and do it for an event that we love. The whole thing was awesome.

SAGMEISTER INC.

WHAT IS THE REASON FOR THE NAME OF YOUR STUDIO?
My deep dislike of funny studio names. The realization that if I had put the word "creative" in the name, there would've been not another creative thought possible in that studio (as amply proven by all the studios that did). Ego.

HOW LONG HAVE YOU HAD A STUDIO?
Eighteen years.

HOW MANY EMPLOYEES (FULL-TIME AND FREELANCE)?
Two designers and two interns plus myself. No account service people, accountants, or secretaries.

HOW MANY PRINCIPALS AND EMPLOYEES ARE DESIGNERS?
Everybody at the studio is a designer.

OTHERS?
None.

DO YOU HAVE A STRATEGIST OR ACCOUNT PERSON ON STAFF?
No.

DESCRIBE YOUR CLIENTELE.
Very mixed now: From very large corporations like BMW and Levis, to cultural/educational entities like Columbia University and Les Art Decoratifs in Paris, to charities like Safepoint. And a whole bunch of self-initiated projects like our current documentary project, *The Happy Film*.

ARE YOU ATTEMPTING TO BROADEN YOUR CLIENT BASE?
We always try to get active in new fields because otherwise we get bored, which is not good for our audiences and clients.

DO YOU SPECIALIZE? OR GENERALIZE?
Seventeen years ago we specialized in doing work for the music industry, which was a whole lot of fun for a while before it became stale. Now we try to not concentrate on a single direction.

ARE YOU PRIMARILY PRINT OR VIRTUAL, OR BOTH?
We are 70 percent print and 30 percent virtual.

WHAT PROMPTED YOU TO START A STUDIO?
Tibor Kalman closed M&Co. in order to move to Rome and work on *Colors* magazine full-time. Having worked there, at my favorite studio, it made no sense to look for a job with my second-favorite studio. Starting my own made sense.

HOW DID YOU DETERMINE WHERE YOUR STUDIO WOULD BE LOCATED?
Real estate pressures. I had found a great place that allowed for the studio downstairs and the living upstairs. We stayed in that location for fourteen years.

DESCRIBE YOUR AESTHETIC, STYLISTIC (EVEN PHILOSOPHIC) APPROACH TO DESIGN.
I am still concerned with design that has the ability to touch the viewer's heart. We see so much profes-

PRINCIPALS
STEFAN SAGMEISTER
JESSICA WALSH

FOUNDED
1993

LOCATION
NEW YORK, NY

EMPLOYEES
5 FULL-TIME

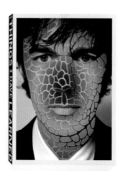

sionally done and well-executed graphic design around us, beautifully illustrated and masterfully photographed; nevertheless, almost all of it leaves me (and I suspect many other viewers) cold.

Our (rarely reached) goal is to touch somebody's heart with design.

HOW MUCH FREEDOM DO YOU ALLOW INDIVIDUAL DESIGNERS?

As we go along, more and more: Like many designers who have been doing this for a while, my need to have my own stamp on every project is largely diminished.

HOW WOULD YOU DEFINE COLLABORATION AS PRACTICED IN YOUR STUDIO?

We work on concepts individually and together. Then we execute them individually and together, with one designer taking on the overall ownership of the project with others chipping in.

COULD YOUR STUDIO GET ALONG WITHOUT YOU FOR ANY PERIOD OF TIME?

Yes, in fact it did this year when I was in Indonesia for the documentary project for three months, and the studio, under Jessica Walsh's leadership, did rather well.

DO YOU HAVE A LONG-TERM PLAN FOR SUSTAINABILITY OR GROWTH?

We usually get far more projects offered than we could take on, but growth has never been on my mind. The fact that we never grew might be my proudest business achievement.

WHAT IS THE MOST CHALLENGING PART OF HAVING A STUDIO?

Figuring this out, how not to grow. The rest is easy.

DESCRIBE THE MOST SATISFYING PROJECT(S) OF THE PAST YEAR.

I'd say the rebranding for EDP, the Portuguese electricity utility who was in many ways an ideal client: They have an excellent product; 60 percent of all the energy they produce right now is renewable. Their CEO, Antonio Mexia, provides clear leadership, and we had access to him for all important decisions. They had a proper budget and timeline.

I had always thought that a small, efficient company like ours could do a wonderful job for a very large corporation, as we can see their world from a more singular and focused point of view. I was right.

The results got fantastic reviews from the audience and the client alike.

(TOP) *Obsessions make my Life worse and my Work better.* DESIGN: Stefan Sagmeister (BOTTOM) *Things I have learned in my life so far.* CONCEPT: Stefan Sagmeister DESIGN: Stefan Sagmeister & Matthias Ernstberger PHOTO: Henry Leutwyle ILLUSTRATION: Yuki Muramatsu, Stephan Walter EDITOR: Deborah Aaronson PRODUCTION: Anet Sirna-Bruder CLIENT: Abrams Inc. DATE: 2008

Douglas Gordons' exhibition "The Vanity of Allegory" at the Guggenheim Museum in Berlin **ABOUT:** Packaged as postcards into a portable box. The cover incorporates a slanted mirror, thus creating vain, reflected typography **CONCEPT:** Stefan Sagmeister **DESIGN:** Stefan Sagmeister and Matthias Ernstberger **PHOTO:** Henry Leutwyle **ILLUSTRATION:** Yuki Muramatsu, Stephan Walter **EDITOR:** Deborah Aaronson **PRODUCTION:** Anet Sirna-Bruder **CLIENT:** Abrams Inc. **DATE:** 2008

Everybody always thinks they are right **DESIGN AND TYPOGRAPHY:** Stefan Sagmeister, Matthias Ernstberger **ILLUSTRATION:** Monika Aichele **PRODUCTION:** Joel Mangrum, Sportogo Inc. **CLIENT:** Six Cities Design Festival, Scotland **COORDINATION:** Ailsa MacKenzie, Stephen Roe, Stuart Gurden **DOCUMENTARY PHOTOGRAPHY:** Inverness: John Paul; all other cities: Mark Hamilton **DATE:** 2007 **SIZE:** Various; six giant inflatables

SAWDUST

PRINCIPALS
ROB GONZALES
JONATHAN QUAINTON

FOUNDED
2006

LOCATION
LONDON

EMPLOYEES
2 FULL-TIME

WHAT IS THE REASON FOR THE NAME OF YOUR STUDIO?

We liked the way it connotes crafts-manship. Sawdust is the by-product of material being crafted, molded, or formed. We like to think of Sawdust as the by-product of our design output.

WHAT PROMPTED YOU TO START A STUDIO?

Meeting Rob at college in Oxford many years back now would be one of the reasons. We became good friends and would always collaborate on projects together; it was a bit of a pipe dream back then but as time went on and we grew in confidence we threw caution to the wind and went for it.

HOW DID YOU DETERMINE WHERE YOUR STUDIO WOULD BE LOCATED?

Due to the size of our studio, we realized that it would help us to be situated in a vibrant creative commu-nity where we would be surrounded by other design companies and like-minded people. We found that Shoreditch, East London ticked the boxes.

DESCRIBE YOUR AESTHETIC, STYLISTIC (EVEN PHILOSOPHIC) APPROACH TO DESIGN.

Our aesthetics or style have usu-ally come through the passion we have for typography, whether it is a logotype or bespoke type treatment, we always try to keep an open mind with the work we do to step away from the "conventional." We focus heavily on the creative concepts, the experience, and interaction as well as the aesthetics.

DO YOU HAVE A STRATEGIST OR ACCOUNT PERSON ON STAFF?

No.

DESCRIBE YOUR CLIENTELE.

Music, art, culture, fashion, corpo-rate, and advertising companies.

ARE YOU ATTEMPTING TO BROADEN YOUR CLIENT BASE?

Yes, a great deal of our work comes project by project and there's no rea-son why we should restrict ourselves to certain types of clients, especially when our work is very adaptable.

DO YOU SPECIALIZE? OR GENERALIZE?

We specialize in creative visual communication involving typography, illustration, and image-making. We admire design that breaks free from convention whilst attaining value on a commercial platform.

ARE YOU PRIMARILY PRINT OR VIRTUAL, OR BOTH?

Neither hold any restrictions to our ideas and creativity so we work across both.

(TOP) Jonathan Quainton **(BOTTOM)** Rob Gonzalez

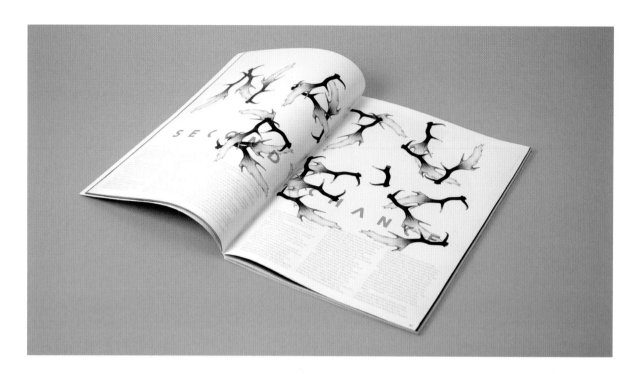

"Nature's Second Chance" **CLIENT:** *Who's Jack* magazine **ABOUT:** Typographic illustration and editorial spread design for "Nature's Second Chance," an article about the rise in popularity of taxidermy as an art form. **DESIGNERS:** Rob Gonzalez, Jonathan Quainton **ILLUSTRATION/TYPE DESIGN:** Rob Gonzalez, Jonathan Quainton **DATE:** 2012

HOW MUCH FREEDOM DO YOU ALLOW INDIVIDUAL DESIGNERS?

As long as there is a clear objective to the communication and direction then the designer should be given complete freedom to do what they do best. To get the best from designers we have to leave them to immerse themselves in the project and experiment—without this freedom you can't explore new ideas.

HOW WOULD YOU DEFINE COLLABORATION AS PRACTICED IN YOUR STUDIO?

For small studios like Sawdust, collaboration can be very important and an exciting prospect. It can evolve in new directions and create extremely diverse work that wouldn't be achieved alone. Working alongside other creatives can arouse a lot of attention in the creative community, especially if it brings something unexpected into the world.

COULD YOUR STUDIO GET ALONG WITHOUT YOU FOR ANY PERIOD OF TIME?

As Rob and I take up a few different roles in the internal runnings of the studio, I could only imagine that things would soon get neglected if one of us were missing for too long. As for the work produced, it would get a great deal harder to get things done as quickly as we seem to motivate each other and push the quality of work to higher levels.

DO YOU HAVE A LONG-TERM PLAN FOR SUSTAINABILITY OR GROWTH?

Only to grow our knowledge of the industry, but at the moment we plan to stay as a duo.

WHAT IS THE MOST CHALLENGING PART OF HAVING A STUDIO?

Running the studio from day to day and assigning enough time to produce good work. Time is definitely at a premium.

DESCRIBE THE MOST SATISFYING PROJECT(S) OF THE PAST YEAR.

The NewModern typeface that we produced for HypeForType was very well received last year. This was an enjoyable project for us to complete, as it was the first fully usable typeface that we had created. When this was made available to buy we had a very positive response, and it was really nice to see other people using our typeface in their work.

(TOP) "This is Now" poster **CLIENT:** Oh Yeah Studio **ABOUT:** Poster created for "This is Now" exhibition, Oslo, Norway. Curated by Oh Yeah Studio. **DATE:** 2012 **DESIGNERS:** Rob Gonzalez, Jonathan Quainton **COPYWRITERS:** Quote by János Bolyai **ILLUSTRATION/TYPE DESIGN:** Rob Gonzalez, Jonathan Quainton **(BOTTOM)** *We All Live Underground* **CLIENT:** Studio project **ABOUT:** A studio project exploring the possibilities of a typeface that uses a very strict set of shapes—in this case a red circle and blue bar, recognizable as the London Underground symbol. **DESIGNERS:** Rob Gonzalez, Jonathan Quainton **COPYWRITERS:** Rob Gonzalez, Jonathan Quainton **ILLUSTRATION/TYPE DESIGN:** Rob Gonzalez, Jonathan Quainton **DATE:** 2012

344 DESIGN, LLC

PRINCIPAL
STEFAN BUCHER

FOUNDED
1998

LOCATION
LOS ANGELES, CA

EMPLOYEES
1 FULL-TIME

WHAT IS THE REASON FOR THE NAME OF YOUR STUDIO?

The studio is located at the merger of the 134 and 210 Freeways in Los Angeles. A few years into the journey I also realized that the three hundred and forty-fourth day of the year (in a non-leap year) is the day I moved from Germany to California—a day I still celebrate as my U.S. birthday.

HOW LONG HAVE YOU HAD A STUDIO?

Since 1998.

HOW MANY EMPLOYEES (FULL-TIME AND FREELANCE)?

I'm the lone full-time employee. Once in a blue moon I take on some equally lone outside contractors for specific tasks such as developing an app or a website with me.

HOW MANY PRINCIPALS AND EMPLOYEES ARE DESIGNERS?

All one of them.

DO YOU HAVE A STRATEGIST OR ACCOUNT PERSON ON STAFF?

I do it all myself, because I'm a control freak and also stupid.

DESCRIBE YOUR CLIENTELE.

This year alone I've written and illustrated two books, designed a bunch of high-end art catalogs, created the typography for a $100 million swords-and-sandals movie, given life to a plush Yeti for Saks Fifth Avenue, and I'm now designing theater façades for the Blue Man Group. The one common thread that connects my clients is that they all live for what

they're doing, and that they love making beautiful things with a fellow lunatic. Everything is "Yes, and..."

ARE YOU ATTEMPTING TO BROADEN YOUR CLIENT BASE?

No. Not at all. I've tried reaching out, making calls, finding clients I think will suit me—all to no avail. For better or worse, I rely on people to find me. My business thrives when I simply make the things I want to make. The other crazies always see and understand, and when they need my help they know how to reach me.

DO YOU SPECIALIZE? OR GENERALIZE?

I'm highly specialized in the kind of work I do—it's pretty much all personal work—and extremely general when it comes to media and clients.

ARE YOU PRIMARILY PRINT OR VIRTUAL, OR BOTH?

By choice, it's been mostly print for the past fifteen years, but there's now more and more virtual work involved—film, video, the app, a tiny bit of web work here and there, some architectural bits, plush. I like new surfaces.

WHAT PROMPTED YOU TO START A STUDIO?

I'm a horrible employee. In an existing hierarchy I immediately get into a major internal conflict between wanting to please my superiors and making exactly what's in my head no matter what anybody tells me. I'm completely blind to office politics. I don't work well on a nine-to-five

(LEFT) **PHOTO:** Linda Abbott **(ABOVE)**
An unvarnished look at my office in
the late afternoon. **(RIGHT)** The Saks
Fifth Avenue Yeti **CLIENT:** Saks Fifth
Avenue **CHARACTER DESIGN:** Stefan G.
Bucher **CONCEPT:** Pentagram London
SNOWFLAKE DESIGN: Marian Bantjes
CREATIVE DIRECTION: Terron Schaefer
ART DIRECTION: Christopher Wieliczko

344 Questions: The Creative Person's Do-It-Yourself Guide to Insight, Survival, and Artistic Fulfillment **CLIENT:** New Riders **TEXT AND ILLUSTRATION:** Stefan G. Bucher **DATE:** 2011

schedule. I'm too damn chatty, and don't get anything done with people around. It's just not a good fit. But when I can just sit alone at my desk everything comes together beautifully. Having a studio is a respectable way of being a hermit/crackpot.

HOW DID YOU DETERMINE WHERE YOUR STUDIO WOULD BE LOCATED?
I fell in love with the view.

DESCRIBE YOUR AESTHETIC, STYLISTIC (EVEN PHILOSOPHIC) APPROACH TO DESIGN.
Over the years I've tried aligning myself with various styles and approaches, because there's real comfort in going with the flow. It never worked. I don't want to be flip about it, but I just do what I do. Of course I pay attention to what's going on around me, and it clearly finds its way into my work, but sometimes it takes a day and sometimes it takes ten years to become visible. It's like doing a forensic analysis on a pot of stew while it's still cooking. Everything always ends up looking like my stuff anyway. I'm a bad mimic.

My design philosophy, such as it is, comes down to treating each assignment as its own set of data, and finding the shape that that particular set wants to take. My goal is always to make the result feel natural and inevitable. The thing should just look like it's supposed to look.

HOW MUCH FREEDOM DO YOU ALLOW INDIVIDUAL DESIGNERS?
Any help I get tends to be fairly technical. I've asked people for creative contributions, but they rarely fit. Most people just don't get as obsessed about the job as I do. That says nothing about their talent or their skills, but when it comes to putting everything into the work, they've almost all had healthier boundaries than me. And I can't work with that.

HOW WOULD YOU DEFINE COLLABORATION AS PRACTICED IN YOUR STUDIO?
It isn't.

COULD YOUR STUDIO GET ALONG WITHOUT YOU FOR ANY PERIOD OF TIME?
No. It would cease to exist. I'm working on a contingency plan if I should ever get seriously ill or have an accident. I've set aside reserves, but in terms of the ongoing work, I'd be completely screwed. It's a major weakness that I haven't addressed.

DO YOU HAVE A LONG-TERM PLAN FOR SUSTAINABILITY OR GROWTH?
With any luck I'll be sitting here until the day I keel over. I work out and eat well. The studio exists solely to let me do my work. It doesn't have to grow or survive beyond that.

WHAT IS THE MOST CHALLENGING PART OF HAVING A STUDIO?
There is never a moment when I feel that I've done everything I could. There is always something else that I could add or improve. I'm not so great at letting things go. 344 is my obsession, and obsessions don't have an "off" switch.

DESCRIBE THE MOST SATISFYING PROJECT(S) OF THE PAST YEAR?
Earlier this year I was invited to design a plush Yeti for Saks Fifth Avenue, and I ended up designing the character, writing and illustrating a twenty-page booklet about his emotional care, and designing a custom carrying pouch and all kinds of historical documentation for him. He's got a whole little world now, and creating worlds is always the most fun assignment. They exist in my head anyway, so it's brilliant when clients ask me, "Hey, what's around that corner?"

The Daily Monster® Monster Maker app
DESIGN AND ILLUSTRATION: Stefan G. Bucher
DEVELOPMENT: Dominik Wei-Fieg

STUDIO LAUCKE SIEBEIN

PRINCIPALS
**JOHANNA SIEBEIN
DIRK LAUCKE**

FOUNDED
2000

LOCATIONS
**AMSTERDAM
& BERLIN**

EMPLOYEES
4 FULL-TIME

WHAT IS THE REASON FOR THE NAME OF YOUR STUDIO?

It is difficult to find the right name for a studio, especially in the beginning of a career. When we established our own studio twelve years ago, naturally we didn't have a body of work to build on. Probably that was the reason that all the potential studio names on our long list sounded kind of silly. Eventually we realized that all the design studios that we admired at the time actually all had rather random names, sometimes even stupid ones, and that it was the fantastic work of these studios that made one fancy their names. So to make a long story short, Laucke and Siebein seemed to be two names that we could charge with positive associations in the same way easily, as long as we managed to deliver great work. Later we added the word "studio" because it implies that other designers could work for us as well.

HOW LONG HAVE YOU HAD A STUDIO?

Since 2000.

HOW MANY EMPLOYEES (FULL-TIME AND FREELANCE)?

Right now we employ two designers.

HOW MANY PRINCIPALS AND EMPLOYEES ARE DESIGNERS?

Everyone who works for us is a fully educated designer. We answer the telephone ourselves, do the bookkeeping, and supervise the production.

OTHERS?

None.

DO YOU HAVE A STRATEGIST OR ACCOUNT PERSON ON STAFF?

No, design is strategy already.

DESCRIBE YOUR CLIENTELE.

Our portfolio of clients is a rather versatile one. We work for multinationals like Akzo Nobel, for national companies in the textile industry, and for various institutions in the contemporary art and cultural sectors. We are proud of this bandwidth. Commissions related to the cultural field are often badly paid. Thanks to our work for clients like Akzo Nobel, however, we can afford to take them on. At the same time, those big clients profit from the kind of refined and exclusive (in a good sense) work that we for instance produce for artists. The high endurance and ability to critically reflect involved in these kinds of cultural commissions benefit our big clients. We feel that in the world of multinationals, graphic design is too often thought about in an ephemeral and one-dimensional way.

ARE YOU ATTEMPTING TO BROADEN YOUR CLIENT BASE?

Unfortunately, we are a bit sloppy about this.

DO YOU SPECIALIZE? OR GENERALIZE?

Both! We believe that certain aspects of communication are universal. On the other hand, we are conscious of the fact that we have not mastered certain areas as well as others. We are primarily interested in reason and not so much in seduction.

Corporate design for the Swiss architects Holzer Kobler Architekturen. **ABOUT:** The typography of the identity—referencing movie posters and end credits—was inspired by the firm's multidisciplinary work, which is often driven by scenic storytelling. Includes stationery, portfolio, website, poster, signage. **DATE:** 2011

ARE YOU PRIMARILY PRINT OR VIRTUAL, OR BOTH?

Originally, exclusively print. However, we make a considerable part of our revenue through virtual products. Apparently we are quite good at that as well.

WHAT PROMPTED YOU TO START A STUDIO?

Somebody who works for someone else never directly and truly gets credit for what he or she is doing. He or she is sort of a random presence in the particular office that got the commission. Of course the client trusts that someone reasonable and competent will work on the assignment, but as soon as difficulties arise—and in design it's very likely they will at some point—clients start to ask: Well, what does the boss think of this?

We didn't like this situation and decided to work under our own names.

HOW DID YOU DETERMINE WHERE YOUR STUDIO WOULD BE LOCATED?

Amsterdam: Randomly. We happen to live there, and a studio was available.

With our branch in Berlin it was a conscious decision. We believe that in the near future there will be a lot of work in Germany. The Netherlands suffer a bit from depression at the moment.

DESCRIBE YOUR AESTHETIC, STYLISTIC (EVEN PHILOSOPHIC) APPROACH TO DESIGN.

Clearly, to answer this question properly many pages of blank paper would be needed. Our ideas about design are in constant transition and are the product of a process of evolving insights. In general, one could say that in the best sense we

feel somewhat obliged to modernism in the way that we try to find meaningful answers to specific design problems. Of course it is always about communication but also about the production means available to us, like time and money, which naturally influence our solutions. Fashion and good taste don't actually interest us that much.

HOW MUCH FREEDOM DO YOU ALLOW INDIVIDUAL DESIGNERS?

All the freedom necessary to get to a good result that meets the goals of the assignment. If we have a feeling that someone working for us has his own agenda and is concerned about his portfolio more than the needs of the client, we will be very, very unforgiving.

HOW WOULD YOU DEFINE COLLABORATION AS PRACTICED IN YOUR STUDIO?

Concept development is a collective activity. On a formal level everybody stands his own ground. We are good craftsmen and can transform an idea into an appropriate form individually. Many roads lead to Rome. Why should we get on each other's backs over that?

COULD YOUR STUDIO GET ALONG WITHOUT YOU FOR ANY PERIOD OF TIME?

No, because if one of us is gone the studio is practically empty.

DO YOU HAVE A LONG-TERM PLAN FOR SUSTAINABILITY OR GROWTH?

Growth, negative. Sustainability, absolutely. We believe in internationalization. A considerable part of the graphic designer's work has either vanished or been automated or marginalized. We will for sure need to travel further in the future to find intelligent people.

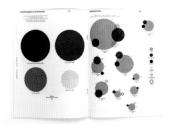

2009 annual report for the Dutch foundation for cultural projects SNS REAAL Fonds. **ABOUT:** A linen cover holds together separate dossiers dealing with the organization, statistics, the sponsored projects, interviews, etc. **DATE:** 2010

WHAT IS THE MOST CHALLENGING PART OF HAVING A STUDIO?

Delivering good work is the only challenge that we are interested in. Everything else is incidental, not a challenge.

DESCRIBE THE MOST SATISFYING PROJECT(S) OF THE PAST YEAR.

Real satisfaction with a product doesn't come until long after a product has been finished and we can see that everything really functions properly, the way we intended it. The series of invites for the Berlin gallery ScheiblerMitte is such a case. We developed a few rules of course, which is the very essence of design—to establish the rules of the game. Of course one never does know for sure whether there might be a miscalculation somewhere. For example: In a graphic appearance, a corporate identity, the notion of "series" plays an important role. Not all possibilities of the game can possibly unfold in the first round that is the product. Often, much effort is put into the concept of the serial character, whereas later it seems that what was intended as a series will stop after one, two, or three issues for various reasons that lie outside of the design process. For ScheiblerMitte we just designed over twenty invites that function perfectly as individual designs. When we reviewed the entire series later we were absolutely euphoric about the entity as a series as well.

ScheiblerMitte

ScheiblerMitte · Charlottenstraße 2 (in der Durchfahrt), 10969 Berlin

Michel Auder · Heads of the Town · ScheiblerMitte · 7. Februar–7. März 2009

ScheiblerMitte

David Robilliard/Christian Holstad · 14. März–18. April 2009 · Eröffnung: 13. März 2009/18–21 Uhr

ScheiblerMitte

The Outward Urge

Eröffnung:
5. September 19–21 Uhr
Dauer:
6. September–18. Oktober 2008

Trouble with Lician
2008, Öl auf Leinwand, 193,5 x 153 cm

ScheiblerMitte

11. September – 16. Oktober 2010
Eröffnung
10. September 2010 18–21 Uhr

ScheiblerMitte
6. Februar–1. April 2010
Eröffnung
5. Februar, 18–21 Uhr

Thomas Rentmeister
Der Staatsanwalt

Anthony Goicolea

ScheiblerMitte
1. Mai–3. Juli 2010
Eröffnung
30. April 18–21 Uhr

Series of invitations for the Berlin-based gallery for contemporary art ScheiblerMitte. **ABOUT:** The diagonal stripes reference relics found at the formerly industrial site where the gallery is located. **DATE:** 2007–2011

TAREK ATRISSI DESIGN

WHAT IS THE REASON FOR THE NAME OF YOUR STUDIO?

I started as a freelancer, and in a few years I built a solid base of clients that knew me by name. When it was time to shift my working model to a small design studio setup, it was logical to keep my name as a main component of it. I was also inspired by designers who adopted the same naming strategy and kept a small studio whose work had a very recognizable style.

HOW LONG HAVE YOU HAD A STUDIO?

The business was registered in 2001 and started as a one-person studio.

HOW MANY EMPLOYEES (FULL-TIME AND FREELANCE)?

At the moment, we are a team of four full-timers and three part-time freelancers. We occasionally have interns.

HOW MANY PRINCIPALS AND EMPLOYEES ARE DESIGNERS?

Five out of the seven are graphic designers.

OTHERS?

One is a font developer and another is a project manager.

PRINCIPAL
TAREK ATRISSI

FOUNDED
2001

LOCATION
THE NETHERLANDS

EMPLOYEES
**4 FULL-TIME
3 PART-TIME**

DO YOU HAVE A STRATEGIST OR ACCOUNT PERSON ON STAFF?

No, we don't have a strategist or account person in the traditional sense. To a big extent, every designer has to conceptualize and apply the strategy of his own projects, and often serves as the direct point of contact with the client.

DESCRIBE YOUR CLIENTELE.

We have a varied range of clientele, but generally speaking our clients are mostly in the cultural sector: museums, educational institutions, and nonprofit, cross-cultural organizations. We have a lot of small businesses and startups that come to us for a complete branding solution (print and web). On the other hand, our large clients, such as telecom companies and multinationals, often come our way for custom Arabic or bilingual type design. The variety of types of clients makes things easier from a creative and business point of view. It helps that our clients are international and not located in one specific market.

ARE YOU ATTEMPTING TO BROADEN YOUR CLIENT BASE?

Indirectly we are. We jump at every market or technological development to bring our expertise to it. We have been very active, for example, with the rise of the iPad, in exploring the possibilities of Arabic design in application developments. We work then on widening our expertise and hence opening doors to offer new solutions to our existing clients, and to new potential clients.

DO YOU SPECIALIZE? OR GENERALIZE?

Both. My studio is specialized in Arabic typography and multilingual and cross-cultural communication. It is a very defined specialization, yet it allows a broad range of diversified work. A focus on Arabic typography could mean a font design development, a TV graphics-branding package, or designing graphics for a museum exhibition.

ARE YOU PRIMARILY PRINT OR VIRTUAL, OR BOTH?

Both. Any medium involving typography falls within our multidisciplinary services. Today, as a small design studio, I think it is wiser to be multidisciplinary.

WHAT PROMPTED YOU TO START A STUDIO?

The Arab world was largely dominated by large advertising agencies that were often doing mediocre design work. There was a lack of "design-studio" culture, and this was the main motivation behind starting my studio. I started my studio with the goal of providing high-level design produced in a small design studio.

HOW DID YOU DETERMINE WHERE YOUR STUDIO WOULD BE LOCATED?

My decision in determining the location of my studio was very practical: I lived, worked, and studied in five different countries that were all locations I could potentially settle in: Lebanon, New York, the Netherlands, Qatar, and Dubai. Eventually I decided to set up my studio in the Netherlands because it was centrally located and offered a good overall package. Being based in Holland nourishes my studio's cross-cultural approach to design, not to mention the fact that the Netherlands is one of the most influential countries in design in the world, with a particularly long and rich tradition in typography and graphic design. On the other hand, since the Arab world is geographically so large and has

All designs by Tarek Atrissi Design (www.atrissi.com)

many intercultural differences, being outside the Arab world helps me and my studio look objectively at the Arab region entirely, and research aesthetic trends and design conventions in the Arab world.

DESCRIBE YOUR AESTHETIC, STYLISTIC (EVEN PHILOSOPHIC) APPROACH TO DESIGN.

My design style is minimal, typographic, conceptual, and constantly engaged in finding innovative ways to mix East and West. As a designer, I am always trying to reflect the most accurate image of the Arab world: reflecting the culture, people, streets, and cities of the Arab world today, inspired by a long historical tradition, and expressed in a contemporary spirit.

HOW MUCH FREEDOM DO YOU ALLOW INDIVIDUAL DESIGNERS?

It really depends on the project. Funnily enough, it is when we are working on the small project with a very small budget (or no budget at all) that we allow ourselves the most freedom. That is probably why we take such projects from the start. When you are not fairly compensated financially, you try to allow as much creative freedom as possible.

HOW WOULD YOU DEFINE COLLABORATION AS PRACTICED IN YOUR STUDIO?

There are two levels of collaborations: internal and external.

Internally, this is quite rich, as almost every one of us has a different nationality, cultural background, and work experience. Each person likes focusing on different angles within a project, whether it is attention to color, usability, target groups, or the technical aspect of managing a project. When we sit around and discuss all this together, we each bring our own expertise and point of view to the table. Alternatively, some projects can be taken from start to finish by a single person, but even in those cases, we do kick it around among ourselves a few times to collect fresh input and perspective.

Externally, there are a lot of projects that we work on as part of a bigger team. In those cases, we are a part of a whole, where each team specializing in a certain field brings their expertise to the table. This is of course very enriching for us as a small independent studio, and we have really learned the most when collaborating with people from other fields, such as architects, scenographers, and exhibition designers, to list a few.

COULD YOUR STUDIO GET ALONG WITHOUT YOU FOR ANY PERIOD OF TIME?

For a short period of time, yes; I managed to stay away for two months earlier this year when I took some continuing education courses in New York. For a longer period of time, probably not at this stage. It is something we are hoping to change, but it is hard to do with a small design studio business setup.

DO YOU HAVE A LONG-TERM PLAN FOR SUSTAINABILITY OR GROWTH?

I have no immediate plans for significant growth. Personally I have realized that the bigger the team is, the less design work I am able to do, and that of course is less fun; I am a designer by training and passion and I need to make sure that I am designing at least 50 percent of the time. The idea of opening another office outside Holland is always a possibility, because a lot of our clients are international, but we haven't seriously planned this yet—but maybe we

will in the future.

Plans for sustainability are probably the most challenging ones to implement. We have been trying over the last couple of years to systemize our working method—and we have created an Arabic type foundry (at www.arabictypography.com) in order to create a self-running model for distributing our original Arabic fonts.

WHAT IS THE MOST CHALLENGING PART OF HAVING A STUDIO?

The fact that at the end of the day, you are running a business. And that you need to have a strong ability to think in some cases not as a designer but rather as a business manager. I am lucky to be able to juggle these two skills because of my graduate education as a "design entrepreneur" at the MFA design program at the School of Visual Arts in New York.

DESCRIBE THE MOST SATISFYING PROJECT(S) OF THE PAST YEAR.

The most satisfying project we worked on this past year was a commission by the Arab Museum of Modern Arts, Mathaf, to create a custom bilingual font (Arabic and Latin). The brief was out of the box, and resulted in a long and exciting design process that involved a lot of manual lettering work and experimentations with material, handwriting, and brushstrokes. We created a handwritten, script-like font, which in Arabic was very challenging to achieve in a digital typeface context, because the script is connected on a horizontal baseline.

The project was very rewarding because of the visibility it got, but also for two other reasons: On one hand, it was a confirmation that the type of Arabic fonts we have often

focused on developing are in high demand; fonts designed by graphic designers for graphic designers; fonts that have strong characters and that are ideal for usage in corporate design and branding contexts, and that are designed to communicate a very specific mood or message. Moreover, by being asked to take part in visualizing the written voice of Mathaf, we were one way or another given the honor of being part of Arab modern art, typographically speaking at least.

Project by Hala Abdelmalak and Tarek Atrissi

THESUMOF

WHAT IS THE REASON FOR THE NAME OF YOUR STUDIO?

When I set up my independent practice in 2007 I called it Finn Creative, which is rather unimaginative. But I set up my studio pretty quickly—after my rather radical decision to leave my creative directorship position at Saatchi Design, Sydney, and move to Kununurra, one of the most remote towns in Western Australia. I needed a company name but found it surprisingly difficult to settle on anything interesting, or smart. So I reluctantly chose "Finn Creative." However, after a lot of consideration, in mid-2012 I took the decision to rename my studio "TheSumOf." This company name reflects three specific aspects of the studio: 1) "TheSumOf" is the culmination of my nearly two decades as a practicing designer, not just my work since 2007, when I set up my independent practice; 2) TheSumOf allows me to seamlessly include self-initiated projects like *Open Manifesto* and DEISGNerd, which were previously misunderstood by many people as "side-projects" rather than being integral to my practice; and 3) the fact that each project is the sum of everyone involved, including the clients—not just some sole designer.

HOW MANY EMPLOYEES (FULL-TIME AND FREELANCE)?

While I was based in Kununrra (a town of 6,000 people) there were no opportunities to hire any designers. I was the sole designer in town, alongside a good friend who remains the only architect in Kununurra. In early 2010 I relocated to Brisbane and in the last few months have hired an artist/designer on a two-day-per-week contract. Essentially, I now have a studio of 1.4 people.

HOW MANY PRINCIPALS AND EMPLOYEES ARE DESIGNERS?

Both of us are designers.

DO YOU HAVE A STRATEGIST OR ACCOUNT PERSON ON STAFF?

I develop all the strategy for my client projects, as well as all account management and the rest of the business, which is typical of small design practices. However, my contract designer is excellent with systems and processes so some of these tasks have now been handed over to her.

DESCRIBE YOUR CLIENTELE.

I guess you could say my clientele mainly consists of cultural organizations. This has happened more by circumstance rather than by intent. While I was living in Kununurra most of my clients were Aboriginal related, due to Kununurra's location and the organizations that are based there. At the same time I also rebranded

PRINCIPAL
KEVIN FINN

FOUNDED
2007

LOCATION
BRISBANE, AUSTRALIA

EMPLOYEES
**1 FULL-TIME
1 PART-TIME**

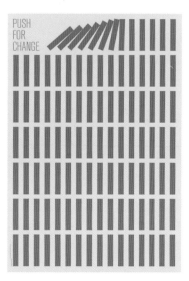

PUSH
FOR
CHANGE

(TOP) *Time* **CLIENT:** Magabala Books
DESIGN: Kevin Finn **ILLUSTRATION:** Kevin
Finn and various **PHOTO:** Ingvar Kenne
and various **DATE:** July 2009 **(BOTTOM)**
Push for Change **CLIENT:** The School
of Visual Arts **DESIGNER:** Kevin Finn
ILLUSTRATOR: Kevin Finn **DATE:** April
2012 **(OPPOSITE)** *Open Manifesto*
DESIGN: Kevin Finn **ILLUSTRATION:**
Kevin Finn **PHOTO:** Kevin Finn **DATE:**
2004–2012

SBS, the most multicultural broadcaster in the world. When I relocated to Brisbane I seemed to gravitate toward cultural organizations again, in particular Brisbane Festival (the Brisbane International Arts Festival) as well as the State Library of Queensland, both of which are now clients. However, I also work with clients who aren't in the cultural sector, but I think there is a more common thread linking all my clients together: I like working with smart, interesting people. But the simple truth is, I'm interested in everything, which allows me to work in any industry or category with smart, interesting people.

ARE YOU ATTEMPTING TO BROADEN YOUR CLIENT BASE?

I am happy moving into any category or industry where there are smart, interesting people operating. However, rather than seeking to broaden my clientele, I have been broadening my output—shifting my practice from a predominantly client-based practice to a practice that also develops its own products. *Open Manifesto* (my independent journal focusing on design culture) was the first foray into this approach many years ago. Last year I created a new brand called DESIGNerd, which aims to celebrate "the design enthusiast." The first product is a series of design trivia games called "100+," featuring personal trivia questions from some of the most significant designers practicing today. The intention is to create a fun, social, and educational tool to further design education and awareness. As a result, I feel certain that I will continue to explore ways to broaden my studio's output, rather than just broadening my client base.

DO YOU SPECIALIZE? OR GENERALIZE?

More often than not, small studios tend to generalize in order to attract as much business as possible in a highly competitive environment. This was my approach at the beginning of my practice. However, due to recent commissions, I have been specializing more and more in strategy-driven design and branding, which is an area I find very stimulating. Over and above this, I'd like to think I specialize in developing ideas, which sounds corny—but ideas are my first area of interest.

ARE YOU PRIMARILY PRINT OR VIRTUAL, OR BOTH?

The majority of my output is print based. When there is a non-print component I contract (or partner with) a specialist in that area. Ideas are transferable to whichever medium is appropriate, and since I place such importance on ideas I feel relatively comfortable working in whichever medium is most suitable. But most of the work I get commissioned to do is either strategic (without a specific designed artefact to produce) or print based—or both.

WHAT PROMPTED YOU TO START A STUDIO?

Necessity. We moved from Sydney because my wife got a job in Kununurra (a ten-hour trip from Sydney—by air). With no other designers or design studios in Kununurra, I had to set up my own practice.

Open manifesto
Some thoughts on graphic design.

{6}

MYTH:
Warren Berger
Andy Chen
Nils Clauss
George Lois
David Miltonberg
Anne Poole
Dean Poole
Pepi Ronalds
Allan Savory
Jason Toelents
Helen Walters
Tom Zoellner

DESCRIBE YOUR AESTHETIC, STYLISTIC (EVEN PHILOSOPHIC) APPROACH TO DESIGN.

I've always tried to avoid developing a signature style of aesthetic. Instead, my hope has been that I might develop an identifiable "style of thinking." Recently, I've come to accept that my style has always been ideas-driven and that my aesthetic is based in "simplicity" (as opposed to being simplistic). It always feels disingenuous to try and answer a question like this, since I believe others might have a more objective view on my body of work. But if we are talking about aspirations, I would dearly like to believe my style is to distill complex issues into simple ideas that can be successfully communicated to a wide audience. That may sound trite, or common, or ridiculous, but I feel this is how my mind operates and, as a result, how my work emerges. Philosophically speaking, I tend to be guided by my personal philosophy: There is wisdom in learning.

HOW WOULD YOU DEFINE COLLABORATION AS PRACTICED IN YOUR STUDIO?

The notion of collaboration underpins my studio name: TheSumOf. Philosophy aside, collaboration is important for project components outside my area of expertise, for example web production, animation, three-dimensional production, photography, illustration, etc. I also tend to approach most of my commissions as collaborations with my clients.

COULD YOUR STUDIO GET ALONG WITHOUT YOU FOR ANY PERIOD OF TIME?

Unfortunately, not at the moment.

DO YOU HAVE A LONG-TERM PLAN FOR SUSTAINABILITY OR GROWTH?

At the moment, I plan to grow my studio output but to refrain from growing the studio size too much. I think having a studio with between three and five people is my studio growth plan over the next few years.

WHAT IS THE MOST CHALLENGING PART OF HAVING A STUDIO?

Having to do everything, from strategy to design to production to account management to production management to accounts to new business, etc.

DESCRIBE THE MOST SATISFYING PROJECT(S) OF THE PAST YEAR.

I feel very fortunate to have been commissioned to rebrand the Brisbane Festival, including designing and producing all the event material for 2011. This instigated a relationship with the organization that is continuing into 2012, which means I can continue contributing to the city's cultural landscape. This is very satisfying. In addition, I am very happy to have launched the DESIGNerd 100+ trivia series. It took about a year from having the idea to launching the final set of products in November 2011. The fact that I was able to achieve this self-initiated project alongside my client commissions has been incredibly satisfying—challenging, but satisfying. And publishing *Open Manifesto* #6 has been incredibly satisfying. It continues to amaze me that *Open Manifesto* provides the opportunity for me to speak with some of the most interesting people on the planet.

(THIS PAGE) SBS **CLIENT:** SBS (the most multicultural broadcaster in the world) **DESIGN/ILLUSTRATION:** Kevin Finn **DATE:** January–May 2008 **(ABOVE OPPOSITE)** DESIGNerd 100+ (graphic design trivia games) **CLIENT:** DESIGNerd **DESIGN:** Kevin Finn **ILLUSTRATION:** Handwritten type by Kevin Finn, Steven Heller, and Stefan Sagmeister **DATE:** November 2011 **(BOTTOM OPPOSITE)** Work In Progress/ The Future Has Past **CLIENT:** The Australia Project **DESIGNER:** Kevin Finn **PHOTOGRAPHER:** Ingvar Kenne **DATE:** January 2010

Mario Fois

Mario Rullo

VERTIGO DESIGN

WHAT IS THE REASON FOR THE NAME OF YOUR STUDIO?

Twelve years ago, when we started looking for a name with Latin roots that would also be understandable to an English-speaking audience, we came across the word "vertigo," in which the theme of dizziness was strongly associated with the theme of creativity.

We love Hitchcock's eponymous film, whose marvelous opening and closing titles by Saul Bass managed to summarize the sense of the film in a few minutes with a continuous and vertiginous flow of images in perfect synchrony with the hypnotic music of Herrmann. A highly suggestive film for all designers.

Twelve years on from that discovery, we are still very satisfied with a name to which, perhaps, we can give some credit for our good luck.

HOW LONG HAVE YOU HAD A STUDIO?

After innumerable experiences as freelance or salaried designers in design studios, communication agencies, and in the sector of exhibition installations, in 1999, we decided to launch ourselves in a new venture.

Thus we brought a wide range of skills that, over time, have enabled us to handle widely different projects and, at the same time, acquire new skills.

HOW MANY EMPLOYEES (FULL-TIME AND FREELANCE)?

Vertigo has five full-time employees and a network of freelance workers and external consultants who enable us to expand the studio's skills and capabilities according to customers' needs.

HOW MANY PRINCIPALS AND EMPLOYEES ARE DESIGNERS?

There are six designers in the studio whose ages range from twenty-eight to forty-six.

OTHERS?

Alessandro performs the role of administrative manager and production coordinator as well as resolving the various small and big problems that beset the office.

DO YOU HAVE A STRATEGIST OR ACCOUNT PERSON ON STAFF?

Vertigo's first rule is never to have a strategic planner or account officer.

The designer must dialogue directly with the customer, understand the latter's requests, and defend his own work. It is tiring, but it is the only way to obtain quality results.

DESCRIBE YOUR CLIENTELE?

We operate in the most variegated sectors—from the aerospace industry to pharmaceuticals, from the public administration to nonprofit organizations, and from perfume to films. Our customers are all major national and sometimes multinational companies.

In dealing with such a varied customer base, we have always been helped by an approach that consists of commencing from the need to communicate a message rather than by an attachment to a particular visual style.

PRINCIPALS
**MARIO FOIS
MARIO RULLO**

FOUNDED
1999

LOCATION
ROME, ITALY

EMPLOYEES
**5 FULL-TIME +
FREELANCERS**

Exhibition designed and mounted at the Ara Pacis in Rome for Telespazio's quinquagenary **AGENCY:** Vertigo Design **CREATIVE DIRECTORS:** Mario Rullo, Mario Fois **OTHER DESIGNERS:** Giorgia Giovannelli, Margherita Vecchi, Massimo Scacco, Simone Peccedi **DATE:** 2011

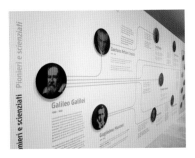

ARE YOU ATTEMPTING TO BROADEN YOUR CLIENT BASE?

For many years, we never needed to look for new customers as they came to us. However, given the current economic crisis that has befallen Italy and the transformation of design and productive dynamics, we need to overhaul our customer base. As probably happens for all companies, we try to present ourselves in the best way possible by earning appreciation for our capacity to listen to and understand our customers' needs and come up with bespoke solutions.

DO YOU SPECIALIZE? OR GENERALIZE?

We like to span all sectors of visual design—identity, branding, publishing, signage, multimedia, exhibits, and packaging—while not forgetting nonconventional advertising and communication.

Vertigo Design has always been characterized by strong eclecticism and conspicuous curiosity. All told, we regard these works as a means to look at the world from a special point of view.

ARE YOU PRIMARILY PRINT OR VIRTUAL, OR BOTH?

As stated before, the particular support for the design is something of great importance to us. What matters most are ideas and the result that they represent. Our designs are both "traditional" and "virtual." While having a close affinity to tradition and to printing, the first web project with which we were involved goes back to 1995. However, when we were invited to a conference on "virtual worlds," we considered it appropriate to underline that visual communication has always worked with virtual. The reason is that, whenever we allude to reality, we have to do so by referring to something fictional.

WHAT PROMPTED YOU TO START A STUDIO?

The desire to deploy a working method based upon design and quality, the care for details, and the search for communicative languages that owe nothing to the fashions of the time.

In addition, we have always dedicated special attention to what we consider fundamental, namely the relationship between text and image, and which, from our beginning, has led us to reflect upon the result of an overall communication.

HOW DID YOU DETERMINE WHERE YOUR STUDIO WOULD BE LOCATED?

Rome is not an easy city for anyone who practices our kind of work, far from industries and with an overly provincial mentality.

But it is the city we love, with two millennia of history and art. And, for this reason, we are always on the lookout for occasions to produce more designs with a public character aimed at culture, the enhancement of the city's amenities, the relationship between citizens, and the city's beauty.

DESCRIBE YOUR AESTHETIC, STYLISTIC (EVEN PHILOSOPHIC) APPROACH TO DESIGN?

We think that the visual designer should have a design method, rather than a predefined style, that enables him on a case-by-case basis to identify the communication language most appropriate for an individual communication work. We believe that a designer must know how to use various expressive techniques, so as to be able to use them in different contexts, and in such a way that every project is functional to the communication objectives and possesses its own original personality.

Tourist itinerary signage in the historic center of Belluno (Veneto, Italy). **ABOUT:** Award-winning project currently being implemented. Signage map with thematic itineraries, infographic and pictographic elements **AGENCY:** Vertigo Design **CREATIVE DIRECTION:** Mario Fois, Mario Rullo **OTHER DESIGN:** Giorgia Giovannelli, Massimo Scacco, Simona Merlini **DATE:** 2011

In certain respects this is a post-modern approach. Today, as a result of the vertiginous development of technology, we can no longer harbour the illusion of an avant-garde that transcends the past to indicate a "path to the future." Instead, any language from any epoch can become the basis for a new and effective project if the objectives and means are clearly stated.

Simply, not a style but a method to be continually updated.

HOW MUCH FREEDOM DO YOU ALLOW INDIVIDUAL DESIGNERS?

All that is necessary to reach the communication strategies defined in the initial briefing.

Vertigo doesn't have a "studio style" that must be slavishly followed. Consequently, the single designers can experiment with the most disparate expressive languages. We are very happy to be able to vary the style of our projects.

HOW WOULD YOU DEFINE COLLABORATION AS PRACTICED IN YOUR STUDIO?

We require our staff to exhibit commitment, concentration and great passion for design work.

Most of our employees and associates have been working with us for many years, often eight or ten years. Ours is a shared developmental path in which we immerse ourselves every day.

COULD YOUR STUDIO GET ALONG WITHOUT YOU FOR ANY PERIOD OF TIME?

The two partners (Mario Rullo and Mario Fois) are concerned with customer management and the creative management of the studio. Therefore, the studio cannot do without at least one of the two figures for long periods of time.

DO YOU HAVE A LONG-TERM PLAN FOR SUSTAINABILITY OR GROWTH?

Our profession requires us (unfortunately or fortunately) to continually redefine our skills and operating arrangements. It is very difficult, therefore, to make long-term plans in a continually changing scenario. Instead, we attempt to intercept and anticipate every new signal around us by attempting to set aside time and space for research and innovation in the communication languages.

WHAT IS THE MOST CHALLENGING PART OF HAVING A STUDIO?

When we concluded our studies and commenced our profession, around 20 years ago, our exclusive concern was to become good designers. When we opened the design studio, we had to learn to be account officers, production managers, talent scouts, teachers, work organizers, and administrators. The time earmarked for design is increasingly eaten up by these obligations. Sometimes we look back to our early days with nostalgia.

DESCRIBE THE MOST SATISFYING PROJECT(S) OF THE PAST YEAR.

We recently won an international competition to design a signage system for the city of Belluno in the north of Italy.

An important design school has entrusted us with the total redefinition of its identity, and the design work is still underway. At present we are concluding the installation of an aerospace exhibition in the prestigious area of the Ara Pacis in Rome. It gives us great pleasure to be able to work on such highly disparate projects that enable us to continue learning something new.

COLLINS:

ESTUDIO MANUEL ESTRADA

HYPERAKT

MORLA DESIGN

PROJECT PROJECTS

SECTION TWO:

MEDIUM FIRMS

9-14 EMPLOYEES

COLLINS:

WHAT IS THE REASON FOR THE NAME OF YOUR STUDIO?
When we launched, there was a deluge of silly agency names. We kept it simple.

HOW LONG HAVE YOU HAD A STUDIO?
Five years.

HOW MANY EMPLOYEES (FULL-TIME AND FREELANCE)?
Twelve, expanding when we get very busy.

HOW MANY PRINCIPALS AND EMPLOYEES ARE DESIGNERS?
Two partners. Ten employees.

OTHERS?
A production manager, managing director, and a technologist.

DO YOU HAVE A STRATEGIST OR ACCOUNT PERSON ON STAFF?
Yes. Our Creative Director and Partner Leland Maschmeyer plays creative and strategy roles when needed. He's won the Jay Chiat Award for strategic excellence many times, including the first Gold Award for Experience Design. So he has chops. In other cases, we work with freelance strategists who report to him. As we see it, strategy should be treated as a creative discipline because it's hard to know where strategy stops and designing begins.

DESCRIBE YOUR CLIENTELE.
We work with a range of global clients, as well as a handful of much smaller ones and a few startups. We like the mix.

PRINCIPAL
BRIAN COLLINS

FOUNDED
2008

LOCATION
NEW YORK, NY

EMPLOYEES
12 FULL-TIME AND FREELANCE

PHOTO: Christopher McLallen

(THIS PAGE) Microsoft Store **CREA-TIVE DIRECTORS:** Brian Collins, John Fulbrook III **DESIGNERS:** Kevin Brainard, Timothy Goodman, Kyle McDonald, Jason Nuttall **EXPERIENCED ARCHITECTS:** Leland Maschmeyer **(ABOVE OPPOSITE)** Advertising Women of New York **CREATIVE DIRECTOR:** Brian Collins **DESIGNER:** Matt Luckhurst **(BELOW OPPOSITE)** Creative Week **CREATIVE DIRECTOR:** Leland Maschmeyer, Brian Collins **DESIGNER:** Matt Luckhurst

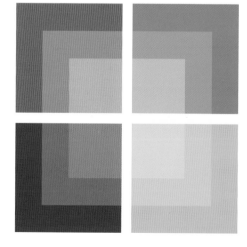

ARE YOU ATTEMPTING TO BROADEN YOUR CLIENT BASE?

Always. Doesn't everyone?

DO YOU SPECIALIZE? OR GENERALIZE?

Generalize. It's like that Q&A session Charles Eames had with Madame L'Amic of the Musée des Arts Décoratifs. L'Amic to Eames: "What are the boundaries of design?" Eames: "What are the boundaries of problems?"

We always feel like we can help in some way. For that reason we've taken on a range of work including communication design, retail design, identity, advertising, packaging, mobile apps, website design, events, and film. Matt Luckhurst just wrote and illustrated his first children's book for Abrams. We'll go wherever curiosity carries us.

ARE YOU PRIMARILY PRINT OR VIRTUAL, OR BOTH?

We focus on developing work that exists in both. Now that doesn't mean we work to make posters that look equally great printed on 24" x 36" and on a 1024 x 768 screen. What it does mean is that we take the idea we intend to deliver and find both the best physical form for it and the best digital, interactive form. The idea is the same, but the expressions are very different.

For Microsoft, we designed the overall store experience from a simple shopping bag to massively complex digital interfaces. It was exhausting, but it was all equally important to us.

WHAT PROMPTED YOU TO START A STUDIO?

It's a bit of that old Buddhist thought that only by exposing ourselves to constant destruction do we find within us that which is indestructible. I had achieved a lot of during my decade at Ogilvy & Mather and loved the people with whom I worked. However, I felt that I needed to learn more. And I feared getting… soft. The best way to fix that was to put myself in the line of fire. So we launched our company, won clients, and learned how to meet a payroll. I've never worked harder. But I've never looked back.

HOW DID YOU DETERMINE WHERE YOUR STUDIO WOULD BE LOCATED?

Union Square? We wanted to be in a vibrant, energetic part of New York that was easy to get to and surrounded by interesting stuff—with good places for food like the Farmer's Market. It's around the corner and keeps us stocked with fresh fruit, vegetables, and far too many home-made strawberry-rhubarb pies.

I've put on ten extra pounds. Not pretty.

DESCRIBE YOUR AESTHETIC, STYLISTIC (EVEN PHILOSOPHIC) APPROACH TO DESIGN

The way I see it, style = accuracy. We create and then execute an idea in a form that drives the best story and creates the biggest outcome.

HOW MUCH FREEDOM DO YOU ALLOW INDIVIDUAL DESIGNERS?

As broad and wide as possible within the structure of the story we wish to tell. It's wide open, really. It's our job to fly cover for gifted, younger designers so they can find their own voice and bring it out in their work. We give them lots of responsibility, early.

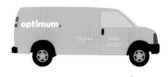

Optimum identity system **CREATIVE DIRECTORS:** Brian Collins, Leland Maschmeyer **DESIGN DIRECTOR:** Matt Luckhurst **DESIGNERS:** Matt Luckhurst, John Custer

HOW WOULD YOU DEFINE COLLABORATION AS PRACTICED IN YOUR STUDIO?

Think *The Muppets Take Manhattan.* The Swedish Chef, Rizzo, Honeydew, Beaker, Kermit, Miss Piggy, Scooter, Sam the Eagle, Sweetums, Dr. Teeth—they all put the fun in dysfunction. That's a good model for us.

Collaboration here is both social and solitary. Some people here are extroverts and love talking all day. Others demand absolute solitude to succeed or nothing good gets made by them. We respect and, more important, protect as many ways of working as there are people.

COULD YOUR STUDIO GET ALONG WITHOUT YOU FOR ANY PERIOD OF TIME?

Absolutely. It sometimes helps that I have more gray hair than others do here. Some clients like that. I, however, could not get along without this team.

I met David Ogilvy early in my career. He offered one piece of advice I never forgot. On recruiting new employees for his agency, he told his partners, "If each of us hires people who are smaller than we are, we shall become a company of dwarfs. But if each of us hires people who are bigger than we are, we shall become a company of giants."

WHAT IS THE MOST CHALLENGING PART OF HAVING A STUDIO?

Balancing the workflow between being overwhelmed and sitting around twiddling thumbs.
DESCRIBE THE MOST SATISFYING

PROJECT(S) OF THE PAST YEAR.

The re-design of Optimum. The big cable company needed to strip away all of the old barnacles and confusion that had grown up around their brand. And they were hell-bent to dramatically improve their products, customer service, and technology experiences. We proposed a radical, almost Spartan simplification of everything they did. And they agreed.

Any company that enthusiastically agrees to paint a big fleet of trucks in our favorite eye-popping colors is our kind of company.

Education
Nation

(TOP) CNN Grill **CREATIVE DIRECTOR:** Brian Collins, John Fulton **DESIGNERS:** Kevin Brainard, Timothy Goodman, John Moon, Jason Nuttall **STRATEGY LEAD:** Leland Maschmeyer **(BOTTOM LEFT)** NBC Education Nation **CREATIVE DIRECTORS:** Leland Maschmeyer, Brian Collins **DESIGNER:** Ashley Stevens, Matt Luckhurst **(BOTTOM RIGHT)** WE Campaign **CLIENT:** Al Gore/The Alliance for Climate Protection **CREATIVE DIRECTOR:** Brian Collins **DESIGNERS:** John Moon, Mickey Pangilinan **CREATIVE:** Ty Harper, Raymond McKinney, Sean Riley/The Martin Agency **TYPOGRAPHER:** Chester Jenkins, Village

ESTUDIO MANUEL ESTRADA

WHAT IS THE REASON FOR THE NAME OF YOUR STUDIO?

The nucleus of the studio is formed around designer Manuel Estrada, whose ideas and drawings are the basis for every project. That's why the studio has his name on it.

HOW LONG HAVE YOU HAD A STUDIO?

The studio has celebrated its twentieth anniversary. Throughout this period, the number of people, as well as the size and complexity of the projects, has been steadily increasing.

HOW MANY EMPLOYEES (FULL-TIME AND FREELANCE)?

The studio employs eleven people full-time. And there are another dozen professionals who habitually work with the studio as freelance collaborators.

HOW MANY PRINCIPALS AND EMPLOYEES ARE DESIGNERS?

Of the eleven people that make up the team, six are graphic designers and one is an industrial designer.

PRINCIPAL
MANUEL ESTRADA

FOUNDED
1992

LOCATION
MADRID, SPAIN

EMPLOYEES
11 FULL-TIME
12 FREELANCE

CLIENT: *Spain Gourmetour* 2000–2011 **ABOUT:** Edited by the Spanish Institute of Foreign Trade for the international promotion of Spanish gastronomy, and published in English, German, French, and Spanish. The magazine won the prize for Best Food Magazine at the World Food Media Awards 2010 in Sydney.

WHAT PROMPTED YOU TO START A STUDIO?

I've always liked to draw. I discovered design when I studied architecture, receiving small jobs to create the occasional poster or logo for a team of architects. This discovery led me, along with another four, to form a graphic production group called SIDECAR. For a few years we diligently worked for the most important agencies: Young and Rubicam, JWT, and McCann-Erickson. After five years, I decided that I wanted to get to know and work directly with my customers and to try to pick and choose my own projects. I left the group and alone formed Estudio Manuel Estrada. And this, I believe, was a good idea.

HOW DID YOU DETERMINE WHERE YOUR STUDIO WOULD BE LOCATED?

Europe. Spain. Madrid.

In Spain, the design sector was born somewhat recently and just in the past twenty years has shown strong growth. This coincides with the age of our studio. Spanish design has a close relationship with the design output of our European neighbors, especially Portugal, Italy, France, and Holland. Nevertheless, Madrid is a natural bridge between Europe and Latin America. Madrid is the host of the BID Biennial Latin American of Design (Bienal Iberoamericana de Diseño), now in its third year, and is becoming the Iberoamerican capital of design. Madrid is a European city ranking third in terms of its universities and is a city growing above the national average in spite of the economic crisis. It has fifteen universities and university centers for design, offering degrees in design, a strong Professional Designers Association, and a Public Center of Design, in Matadero,

open to the city. The development of design in Madrid is powerfully linked to the cultural and creative industry that includes museums, foundations, and trade shows. As concerns the publishing and long-standing graphics industry, this is a city with a strong visual culture, involved in cinema, photography, visual arts, and illustration, all of which create a very favorable environment for graphic design.

DESCRIBE YOUR CLIENTELE.

Our studio works for very small companies, very large corporations such as Repsol, which is the leading energy company in Spain, and for public institutions such as the Spanish Ministry of Culture and NGOs. The size of our projects is not as important to us as projects that allow us to be deeply involved in showing just how much design and graphic communication can be expanded.

We generally have a very good relationship with our customers and we try to know everything there is to know about the projects entrusted to us. Without good information, there cannot be good design, and the same holds true for a good customer-designer relationship.

DESCRIBE YOUR AESTHETIC, STYLISTIC (EVEN PHILOSOPHIC) APPROACH TO DESIGN.

Design is an applied art. But it is not a mere decoration. Design is the structural part of objects, every object, whether they are chairs, books, houses, logos, or typefaces. Objects cannot be divided into those with design and those without, but rather into objects that are well thought out or well designed and objects that are ill designed. Design is a committed discipline and cannot be an end in itself. Design can, and must, make

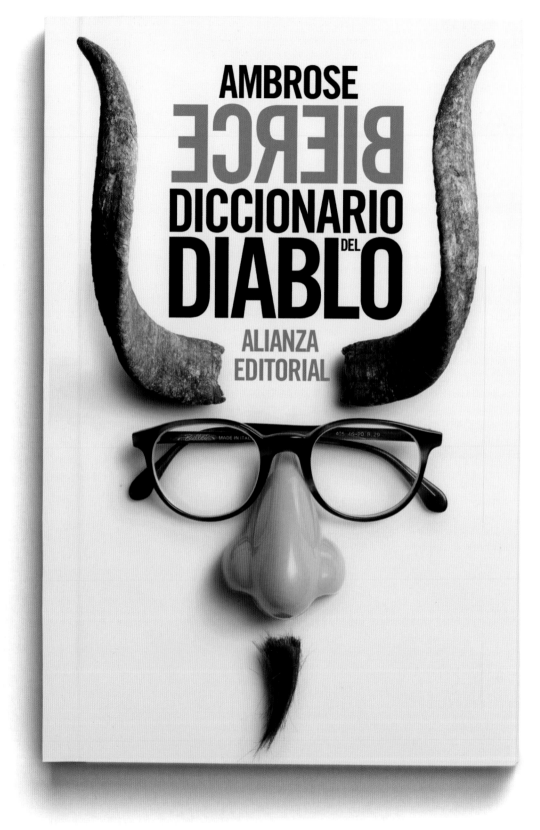

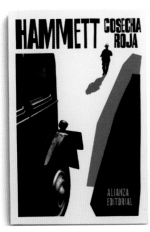

life easy for people. To understand this ethical approach as a limitation to possible design aesthetics is to ignore the enormous functional and emotional scope that some of the greatest milestones of design have had in contemporary culture. The designer is an artist without a pedestal; he must work at the street level, avoiding elitist proposals and understanding that his successes are also due to his customers, who hold on their heads the apple at which we design-archers take our aim.

WHAT IS THE MOST CHALLENGING PART OF HAVING A STUDIO?

It is difficult to reconcile business activity with the carrying out of a creative activity such as design. This has been the main challenge faced by our studio these past few years: to create an organizational structure, financial performance, and customer relationships that ensure everything is in the service of good design.

Many companies find that economic results and turnover are the main objective. This is only secondary for us. Undoubtedly, our primary goal is the search for quality in design. In spite of this, our economic performance in recent years has discreetly improved despite the economic crisis that Spain has been suffering since 2008.

DESCRIBE THE MOST SATISFYING PROJECT(S) OF THE PAST YEAR.

During these recent years we have carried out visual identity and museography projects with some of the most important museums opened in Spain, such as the Museum of Human Evolution in the city of Burgos, the Army Museum in Toledo, the Costume Museum in Madrid, and the Greco Museum, also in Toledo.

We have developed all the corporate communications for Repsol during the past four years, including its paper publications and website. During the last three years, our activity with these extended projects was coordinated with more economic development through the creation of brands and corporate image projects. These years were also marked by intense activity in editorial design, such as the redesign of the paperback book collection for Alianza Editorial, a collection that has a strong tradition of cover design, designing more than a hundred different covers.

Covers and design of the Pocket Collection 2009–2011 **CLIENT:** Alianza Editorial **ABOUT:** Leader in the Spanish book collection market, with a great tradition in the design of their covers. An all-in project, ranging from the design and implementation of all the covers, to the choice of formats, materials, typography, and promotional items.

HYPERAKT

WHAT IS THE REASON FOR THE NAME OF YOUR STUDIO?

It stems from a childhood nickname. The co-founder of the company, Deroy Peraza, was a very hyperactive child. His mother called him "trompo loco," which translates from Spanish to "crazy spinning top." In 2001, when the studio was started, broadband was just taking hold and we knew that the web would be a major part of our future. Interacting with hypertext filled with hyperlinks became mainstream. Hyperakt was a way to connect the concepts of hyperactivity and interactivity, and turn it into an action statement. We decided that spelling it with a *k* instead of a *c* would add some mystery to the equation and would allow us to have a distinguishable name that wouldn't get lost on web searches.

HOW LONG HAVE YOU HAD A STUDIO?

We just celebrated our ten-year anniversary! The studio was founded by Deroy Peraza in September 2002. A year later, Julia Vakser Zeltser joined as a co-founding partner. We were both fresh out of school and in our early twenties.

HOW MANY EMPLOYEES (FULL-TIME AND FREELANCE)?

Eight full-time Hyperaktivists, one full-time intern, two to three freelancers, three development partners.

HOW MANY PRINCIPALS AND EMPLOYEES ARE DESIGNERS?

Eight of nine.

PRINCIPALS
**JULIA VAKSER ZELTSER
DEROY PERAZA**

FOUNDED
2002

LOCATION
BROOKLYN, NY

EMPLOYEES
**15 FULL-TIME AND
FREELANCERS**

OTHERS?

One front-end developer/information architect.

DO YOU HAVE A STRATEGIST OR ACCOUNT PERSON ON STAFF?

No. We're currently in the process of looking for our first project manager. As designers, we all consider strategy to be part of our jobs.

DESCRIBE YOUR CLIENTELE.

We work with clients who are working to make the world a better place. The bulk of our clients are social enterprises, foundations, or non-profits. Additionally, we work with a select group of technology companies and startups, and we also have a few editorial clients.

ARE YOU ATTEMPTING TO BROADEN YOUR CLIENT BASE?

Slightly. We recently completed our first branding project for a museum and would love to work with more cultural institutions.

DO YOU SPECIALIZE? OR GENERALIZE?

We specialize in purpose and generalize in deliverables. We work with brands whose stories can have meaningful impact on people's lives. We tell their stories through the media that fits best for each brand.

ARE YOU PRIMARILY PRINT OR VIRTUAL, OR BOTH?

We are a multidisciplinary studio. Our output this year has been 38 percent print, 34 percent web, 19 percent data visualization, and 9 percent branding. That balance has been very stable throughout our existence, with the exception of data visualization. This area of business has seen a meteoric rise over the last few years and is currently our largest growth area.

WHAT PROMPTED YOU TO START A STUDIO?

After working for short periods at a few design studios and agencies, we hadn't found a culture we could wholeheartedly feel a part of. Studios were either too corporate, too centered around the wishes of one person, or filled with incompetence. We couldn't find the right mix of friendliness, talent, and values in an environment full of people that didn't take themselves too seriously. We decided that the best way to address this was to create our very own studio in which we could work towards our own ideal culture.

Beyond culture issues, creating our own studio allowed us to grow at our own pace and to truly take ownership over our mistakes and successes. We were both very inexperienced when we started, so this proved to be a fast-track to learning all about running a design business.

HOW DID YOU DETERMINE WHERE YOUR STUDIO WOULD BE LOCATED?

We (Julia and Deroy) were working out of Deroy's loft apartment in Carroll Gardens, Brooklyn in 2003. We knew that moving into a real studio space would be an important step for us, but we certainly couldn't afford Manhattan. Brooklyn was more our speed. Luckily, we noticed that the storefront space two doors down from the loft was being renovated. The space had been vacant for twenty years. We found another studio to share the space with and rented it. We have been in the space since early 2004 and took over the full space in 2007.

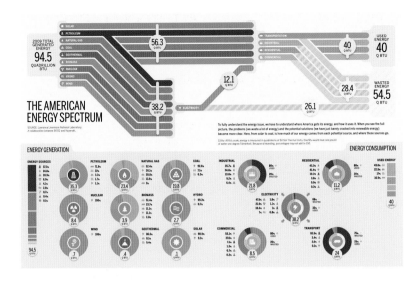

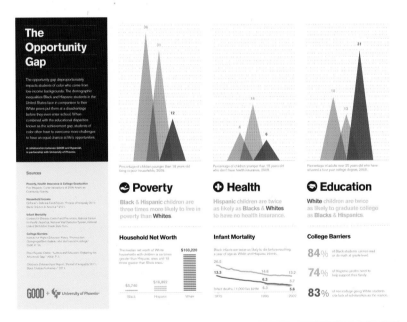

The Opportunity Gap **CLIENT:** *GOOD* Magazine **TYPE:** Infographic **CREATIVE DIRECTION:** Deroy Peraza
DESIGN: Deroy Peraza, Eric Fensterheim, Josh Smith

DESCRIBE YOUR AESTHETIC, STYLISTIC (EVEN PHILOSOPHIC) APPROACH TO DESIGN.

We strive for well-crafted, accessible design with clarity of purpose that is filled with optimism, curiosity, and wonder. Both form and function are balanced at the core of everything we produce and our aesthetic varies widely depending on the project.

We draw our inspiration from many influences:

Julia was born in Ukraine and Deroy in Cuba, so the language of political propaganda has been a source of interest and influence.

Both principals had stints living in Europe during college (Julia in Paris, Deroy in Barcelona and London), which had a huge effect on our visual language and opened our eyes to different design philosophies. In fact six of the nine Hyperaktivists were born outside of the U.S.

Several Hyperaktivists, including the two partners, have illustration backgrounds, which is often evident in our work.

HOW MUCH FREEDOM DO YOU ALLOW INDIVIDUAL DESIGNERS?

We take great care in bringing in talented people who live and breathe design, can identify with our mission, and complement our studio culture. This allows us to give designers a great deal of freedom. Hyperakt is not built to be a temple to its leaders. Everyone is an important part of the studio's voice. We put a lot of trust in the designers so they feel ownership in the work they do and so they are constantly being challenged to grow. Younger designers are mentored by more experienced designers so they can build up the confidence to lead their own projects. As principals, we are working hard to create a studio that is guided by our ideals—creating meaningful design for the common good—but that is not completely dependent on us as individuals.

HOW WOULD YOU DEFINE COLLABORATION AS PRACTICED IN YOUR STUDIO?

The studio atmosphere is extremely laid back, and we work in a small open space where everyone is constantly communicating with each other. Projects teams usually consist of two or three people working together. Works in progress are posted on a wall so everyone can see what everyone else is working on and provide feedback at will. We do informal presentations all the time and hold regular studio meetings on Mondays, so everyone is aware of everything that's happening in the studio. Additionally, we are increasingly dedicating time and resources to developing projects conceived and led by our designers as a way to foster innovation and collaboration.

COULD YOUR STUDIO GET ALONG WITHOUT YOU FOR ANY PERIOD OF TIME?

Yes. For short periods of time. We have designers on the team who are empowered to lead projects, communicate directly with clients, and manage resources. The studio is reliant on the principals for creative direction, new business development, and some administrative operations at the moment, some of which we're addressing. The two partners also have the freedom to take extended leaves or work from different geographic locations. We're good at covering for each other.

DO YOU HAVE A LONG-TERM PLAN FOR SUSTAINABILITY OR GROWTH?

For many years, our plan for sustainability involved working long hours

2010 Annual Report **CLIENT:** Ford Foundation **TYPE:** Print **CREATIVE DIRECTION AND DESIGN:** Josh Smith, Julia Vakser Zeltser, Deroy Peraza **DESIGN:** Wen Ping Huang, Jason Lynch, Aymie Spitzer, Eric Fensterheim

and pouring our hearts and souls into the work to have enough money to pay bills at the end of the month. Not knowing how to break out of that unhealthy cycle, we turned to a consultant, recommended by a friend in the industry, who specializes in design businesses. Over the last few years, she's schooled us on some of the basics and helped us get to a place where we can focus more on the kind of work we want to be doing, and less on covering our expenses. She's had a tremendous impact on our business and has helped us grow from four employees to nine this year.

Our long-term plan is in constant flux as we strive for more creative freedom. As partners, we have regular conversations about our goals and try to remain nimble so we can adapt easily to new opportunities. We'd like Hyperakt to remain small so we can preserve our tight-knit family culture and continue to be involved in all of the studio's creative output.

WHAT IS THE MOST CHALLENGING PART OF HAVING A STUDIO?

There are different sets of challenges at every stage of running a studio. In the early years, when we lacked experience and confidence, we worried about the quality of our work and struggled to learn the basics of administration (billing, taxes, incorporating). Then we struggled to figure out when it was time to hire our first employee, how to manage other people, how to focus the studio's strategy, and how to make the studio financially sustainable.

The most recent challenge we've experienced has been a product of our growth. Transitioning from four to nine full-time employees has been awesome and exciting in every way,

and we are constantly learning. We pay more attention now than ever before to the studio's culture and to the individual goals and needs of each Hyperaktivist. We're working hard to create transparency and to streamline our systems so we're all as efficient as we can be.

Mastering these challenges is one of the most exciting parts of having a studio and running a business. It's incredibly hard and not for the faint of heart, but the sense of accomplishment that comes with each win is tremendous.

DESCRIBE THE MOST SATISFYING PROJECT(S) OF THE PAST YEAR.

We are fortunate in that we get a lot of satisfaction from most of the work we do, so it's hard to choose just one "most satisfying" project. The data visualization work we've done for GOOD over the last year has been incredibly rewarding on many levels. They are a great client to work with and give us a lot of creative freedom. The topics they cover are wide-ranging, align with our vision, and reach an audience that fits us well. But, we've also been lucky to have worked with some fantastic organizations that are impacting the world in powerful ways. We couldn't be prouder to have been involved with the Ford Foundation, UNICEF, Acumen Fund, Collaborative Fund, ClimateWorks, and so many others who are making the world a better place.

Rhetoric Posters **CLIENT:** Hyperakt **TYPE:** Print
CREATIVE DIRECTION AND DESIGN: Deroy Peraza

MORLA DESIGN

WHAT IS THE REASON FOR THE NAME OF YOUR STUDIO?
Clients knew my name and liked my work.

HOW LONG HAVE YOU HAD A STUDIO?
Since 1984.

HOW MANY EMPLOYEES (FULL-TIME AND FREELANCE)?
Depending on the year, anywhere from three to fourteen, some full-time, some freelance, some interns.

HOW MANY PRINCIPALS AND EMPLOYEES ARE DESIGNERS?
Myself plus anywhere from two to ten designers (which could include model builders, architects, and other specialized creatives).

OTHERS?
We have an office manager/production manager and will hire freelance, if necessary, to meet project needs.

DO YOU HAVE A STRATEGIST OR ACCOUNT PERSON ON STAFF?
No.

DESCRIBE YOUR CLIENTELE.
Morla Design is a multi-disciplinary studio and therefore has an eclectic client roster that keeps me engaged in a broad range of work and businesses. Some current client projects include naming and designing every aspect of a new brand launch for Williams-Sonoma, creating a 200-page coffee table book for an iconic package goods company, celebrating its hundredth anniversary, and creating the design and interface for a GPS-based mobile app.

ARE YOU ATTEMPTING TO BROADEN YOUR CLIENT BASE?
Always.

DO YOU SPECIALIZE? OR GENERALIZE?
Since I have been designing for over thirty years, I have specialized experience in a number of diverse categories. Categories include retail, banking, luxury goods, art organizations, and education. Project types include total brand development, language and implementation, store design and construction, catalog and direct channel marketing, book design and publishing, and screen-based design solutions.

ARE YOU PRIMARILY PRINT OR VIRTUAL, OR BOTH?
Both.

PRINCIPAL
JENNIFER MORLA

FOUNDED
1984

LOCATION
SAN FRANSISCO, CA

EMPLOYEES
3-14 FULL-TIME + FREELANCE

WHAT PROMPTED YOU TO START A STUDIO?

Previous to 1984, I worked for PBS designing show openings and identities followed by being hired as Art Director for Levi Strauss & Co. My experience in both print and motion graphics at these two remarkable places, combined with strong working relationships with the executive teams, contributed to a secure client base for the launch of Morla Design.

HOW DID YOU DETERMINE WHERE YOUR STUDIO WOULD BE LOCATED?

From the 1980's until 2008, my studio was located in South Park. At that time South Park, in the South of Market area of San Francisco, was somewhat undiscovered. What it did have was a lovely park, a tight creative community, and the best French Bistro in the city. By the mid-90s it became the epicenter of the dot-com movement. By 2008, the ease of digital communication with clients made me re-think the need for 2000 square feet of space. I relocated my studio to the historic, and very happening, Dogpatch area. The new studio space is a small, contemporary gem with twenty-foot ceilings, designed by my husband, Nilus de Matran. And the best pizza con funghi in the city is just two blocks away.

DESCRIBE YOUR AESTHETIC, STYLISTIC (EVEN PHILOSOPHIC) APPROACH TO DESIGN.

Creating innovative solutions that reflect the spirit of a company or an institution and resonate with their audience in meaningful ways.

Levi's Red Version Jeans Brochure **CLIENT:** The Curious Company/Levi Strauss & Co. **ABOUT:** Historical and contemporary images sandwiched between a laminated chip-board cover and bound with a hunky, aluminum spiral.

HOW MUCH FREEDOM DO YOU ALLOW INDIVIDUAL DESIGNERS?

I give pencil sketches and communicate design language and type direction, then let them work on their own. We reconvene at the point when they feel that enough design progress has been made and then work together on more detailed design refinement.

COULD YOUR STUDIO GET ALONG WITHOUT YOU FOR ANY PERIOD OF TIME?

Not really.

DO YOU HAVE A LONG-TERM PLAN FOR SUSTAINABILITY OR GROWTH?

Hmmm, I know I should but always seem to be too busy to map out a plan.

WHAT IS THE MOST CHALLENGING PART OF HAVING A STUDIO?

Never, ever compromising on design and instilling that goal in every person working on every facet of the job. More pragmatically, keeping the right balance of the amount of work coming into the studio.

AIGA Landor Associates Poster **CLIENT:** AIGA San Francisco Chapter **ABOUT:** Landor Associates asked Morla Design to create an announcement for their upcoming lecture series. The oversized poster illustrates many of the numerous trademarks and corporate identities that Landor has produced. The audience for this AIGA lecture was comprised mainly of students and young design professionals. Our challenge was to make Landor's ubiquitous identities exciting and relevant to this younger audience. **ART DIRECTION:** Jennifer Morla **DESIGN:** Jennifer Morla, Brian Singer **COPYWRITING:** Landor Associates **DATE:** 2003

PROJECT PROJECTS

WHAT IS THE REASON FOR THE NAME OF YOUR STUDIO?
The openness of our name was intended to create a flexible framework that could support a diverse range of production. While our practice is clearly, and happily, a design studio, it's also important to us to incorporate activities such as editing, curating, and publishing into our day-to-day work.

HOW LONG HAVE YOU HAD A STUDIO?
Adam Michaels and Prem Krishnamurthy founded Project Projects in 2004; Rob Giampietro joined as the studio's third principal in 2010.

HOW MANY EMPLOYEES (FULL-TIME AND FREELANCE)?
Including the three principals, we have six full-time staff and a steady, rotating pool of freelancers and interns. We typically have about twelve people in the studio at any given time.

HOW MANY PRINCIPALS AND EMPLOYEES ARE DESIGNERS?
Each principal and employee is a designer, with the exception of our studio manager (and she also contributes to our work through conceptualization, research, and writing).

DO YOU HAVE A STRATEGIST OR ACCOUNT PERSON ON STAFF?
We don't have a designated strategist or account person at our studio. Each project is managed by one of the principals (sometimes multiple principals for larger-scale projects), and everyone at the studio actively discusses projects and engages with clients.

DESCRIBE YOUR CLIENTELE.
We primarily work with clients in the art, architecture, cultural, and educational sectors, though we're always open to working with interesting people in other fields.

ARE YOU ATTEMPTING TO BROADEN YOUR CLIENT BASE?
We're always interested in establishing new working relationships, though this process often happens quite organically, rather than according to a specific strategy.

DO YOU SPECIALIZE? OR GENERALIZE?
We're more specialized than not; however, this is due to consistently trying to do work that we genuinely believe in.

ARE YOU PRIMARILY PRINT OR VIRTUAL, OR BOTH?
Both. Beyond the print/virtual binary, however, we have a particular interest in developing concepts that evolve over the course of multiple media and platforms. For example, in working with the Van Alen Institute to produce The Good Life, we designed the show's identity, then reiterated its content and concept through a website, print materials, motion graphics, and a catalog that structurally echoed the exhibition's thematic sections.

WHAT PROMPTED YOU TO START A STUDIO?
When the studio began back in 2004, Adam and Prem both thought it would be a necessary step towards realizing the work that each had in mind at the time. The studio

PRINCIPALS
ADAM MICHAELS
PREM KRISHNAMURTHY
ROB GIAMPIETRO

FOUNDED
2004

LOCATION
NEW YORK, NY

EMPLOYEES
12

has grown substantially since then while maintaining (as well as expanding upon) the original vision.

HOW DID YOU DETERMINE WHERE YOUR STUDIO WOULD BE LOCATED?

Both Adam and Prem were based in New York when the studio began, so that much was a given. The studio has been located in three different Manhattan locations (first in the Financial District, then the Lower East Side, and now on the Bowery), each chosen according to a variety of factors (cost and convenience being significant). For the work that the studio produces, and the clients that we work with, downtown Manhattan is truly ideal.

DESCRIBE YOUR AESTHETIC, STYLISTIC (EVEN PHILOSOPHIC) APPROACH TO DESIGN.

We tend to treat aesthetics as secondary to concepts—as a result, many of our projects have a heterogeneous feel; our aesthetic approach functions as an outgrowth of our ideas. We employ a range of formal vocabularies across our projects, as based upon our assessment of the situation, its context, and the desires of all involved parties. Over the last eight years, we have had the opportunity to see our projects become more complex and hybrid. The studio is constantly evolving and, we'd like to think, improving.

HOW MUCH FREEDOM DO YOU ALLOW INDIVIDUAL DESIGNERS?

We have a varied set of working processes—everyone seems to find their own balance in completing their work. We consider process to be more integrated than a divide between conceptualization and execution might imply. Each person

at our studio strongly influences the projects that she or he is working on.

HOW WOULD YOU DEFINE COLLABORATION AS PRACTICED IN YOUR STUDIO?

Collaboration is a big part of our process—we guest-edited an issue of *Print* magazine in January 2011, using it as a theme and framing our editorial on a roundtable discussion between artists, designers, and educators that we invited to take part in the discussion. Project Projects is a design studio, but we like to think of our activity as existing beyond conventional client-designer relationships. While we listen attentively to our clients' needs and try to fulfill their desires, we are also proactive about lending our own unique experiences, individual research, and conceptual thinking to each project.

Our efforts for assembling teams of collaborators to achieve the best possible outcome for a scenario has led to our recent venture into the business of publishing, as well. The first two titles in our Inventory Books series—an imprint edited and designed by Adam, and published by Princeton Architectural Press—were expansions of previous projects that were so rich in their original form, we wanted to provide much more information about them to a broader public.

COULD YOUR STUDIO GET ALONG WITHOUT YOU FOR ANY PERIOD OF TIME?

As we've produced more work outside of New York City in recent years, both nationally and internationally, requiring increased amounts of travel, we're happy to have found the studio has enough personnel to continue running well while someone might be out of town. However, all seems to run most smoothly when everyone is in one location.

SALT identity system **CLIENT:** SALT Istanbul **DESIGN:** Project Projects **DATE:** January 2011–ongoing

(ABOVE) Tabletmag.com, for which Project Projects designed both the site and identity in September 2011. (RIGHT) The three Inventory Books series releases to date: IB01: *Street Value: Shopping, Planning, and Politics at Fulton Mall*, IB02: *Above the Pavement—The Farm! Architecture and Agriculture at P.F.1*, IB03: *The Electric Information Age Book: McLuhan / Agel / Fiore and the Experimental Paperback* (all by Princeton Architectural Press, 2012)

DO YOU HAVE A LONG-TERM PLAN FOR SUSTAINABILITY OR GROWTH?

Of those words, we prioritize sustainability, while maintaining an open mind about growth.

WHAT IS THE MOST CHALLENGING PART OF HAVING A STUDIO?

We began the studio to produce design work that we deeply cared about, and we didn't especially anticipate the degree to which we would learn how to run an actual business. While it has been challenging to gain that knowledge, it's also been interesting, as the studio itself has become a project far beyond anything that we ever expected.

DESCRIBE THE MOST SATISFYING PROJECT(S) OF THE PAST YEAR.

Adam: The third book in the Inventory Book series, *The Electric Information Age Book: McLuhan/Agel/ Fiore and the Experimental Paperback*, was my most satisfying, due to the integrated process of research, editing, and design, as well as the extremely interesting subject matter.

Prem: The SALT identity system (and all of its extensions: online, in their exhibition spaces, and through their upcoming electronic publishing initiatives) is a project that has been extremely satisfying over the past year. We had the good fortune to work with SALT nearly from its inception to conceive of how graphic design might play a fundamental role in the institution's mission and ongoing programming. This trust and close dialogue has led to an identity system which is both challenging in the present, and which we can continue to develop with SALT over time.

Rob: *Tablet* magazine, the online journal of Jewish news, culture, and

ideas, has been our client for several years now, but our total overhaul of its site this year was both challenging and deeply satisfying. After winning a National Magazine Award earlier in the year, *Tablet* looked to expand its coverage, adding high-profile columnists and increasing service-related areas of the site, such as parenting, food, and holidays. It has been one of the most complex interactive editorial projects our studio has undertaken, but one that was universally embraced by *Tablet's* growing readership. Giving an audience an even better experience with a site they love is always deeply satisfying.

The Electric Information Age Book: McLuhan/ Agel/Fiore and the Experimental Paperback by Jeffrey T. Schnapp and Adam Michaels (Princeton Architectural Press, 2012)

ANGELINI DESIGN

ART + COM

CARBONE SMOLAN AGENCY

COBLISS HMBE

FUNNY GARBAGE

MUCCA DESIGN

SECTION THREE:

LARGE FIRMS

15+ EMPLOYEES

ANGELINI DESIGN

HOW LONG HAVE YOU HAD A STUDIO?
Angelini Design was founded in
Rome in 1985.

**HOW MANY EMPLOYEES (FULL-TIME AND
FREELANCE)?**
We have twenty-five full-time employ-
ees and fifteen freelancers.

**HOW MANY PRINCIPALS AND EMPLOYEES
ARE DESIGNERS?**
Of the twenty-five full-time employees, fifteen are designers, while of
the fifteen freelancers, seven are
designers.

**DO YOU HAVE A STRATEGIST OR ACCOUNT
PERSON ON STAFF?**
We have an account strategist for
each of our three offices, in Rome,
Turin, and Paris, with whom we
decide and set out specific strategies for each client. Then we have
account managers who handle
affairs on a daily basis for each
single client.

DESCRIBE YOUR CLIENTELE.
Our clients are rather varied and
range from the automobile industry
(Fiat, Lancia, and Peugeot), to the
food and beverage industry (Garofalo, Amarelli, Chin8 Neri), to finance
(Fedeuram, Cartasi) and the cell
phone industry (Wind). And more.

Carlo Angelini and Michele Angelini

PRINCIPALS

CARLO ANGELINI, CEO AND CREATIVE DIRECTOR

PATRIZIA BOGLIONE, CREATIVE DIRECTOR

PATRIZIA TOCCI, ACCOUNT DIRECTOR OF ANGELINI DESIGN ROME

FRANCESCA MITRANGOLO, ACCOUNT DIRECTOR OF ANGELINI DESIGN TURIN

JEAN CHRISTOPHE FAILLA, ACCOUNT DIRECTOR OF ANGELINI DESIGN PARIS

MICHELE ANGELINI AND ANDREA INDINI, CREATIVE DIRECTORS OF ANGELINI DESIGN ATELIER

FOUNDED
1985

LOCATIONS
ROME, TURIN & PARIS

EMPLOYEES
25 FULL-TIME AND 15 FREELANCE

ARE YOU ATTEMPTING TO BROADEN YOUR CLIENT BASE?

We try to broaden our client base every day; however, we're also attentive to customer loyalty and keeping and solidifying the relationships we already have with clients.

DO YOU SPECIALIZE? OR GENERALIZE?

We are "generalizing" because we are branching out towards the web and multimedia, but at the same time we are also "specializing" in the three fields of packaging, design, and web.

ARE YOU PRIMARILY PRINT OR VIRTUAL, OR BOTH?

Angelini Design primarily does print work on brand identity, editorial design, and packaging. For two years now, we've also been increasingly specializing in the virtual, media, and multimedia fields, with projects that entail not just the simple construction of websites, but also, on a larger scale, portals and online magazines. This requires strategic planning with regard to clients and brands and an active engagement on the part of our editorial staff with the daily production of content.

WHAT PROMPTED YOU TO START A STUDIO?

Definitely my natural passion for graphics and design plus a predisposition and "vocation" for this line of work.

HOW DID YOU DETERMINE WHERE YOUR STUDIO WOULD BE LOCATED?

There is no "geographic" strategy to our three offices, but simply a question of business opportunities that then became solid realities.

DESCRIBE YOUR AESTHETIC, STYLISTIC (EVEN PHILOSOPHIC) APPROACH TO DESIGN.

There is no label with which to define our style. Unlike many other agencies, our studio is unique in that it isn't mono-style and doesn't have a set, predefined style. Our stylistic and aesthetic approach is based on the needs of our client and the type of work and context. So for Amarelli, for example, we wanted to recreate a vintage feel, whereas for Lancia TrendVisions, a more modern and experimental project, we decided to take a risk and choose fresher and more innovative solutions.

HOW MUCH FREEDOM DO YOU ALLOW INDIVIDUAL DESIGNERS?

Because of this approach, our designers have full creative freedom. Once the direction of the work has been decided together during brainstorming sessions, our designers can move freely, though of course respecting those parameters of quality, attention to detail, and refinement that distinguish us.

HOW WOULD YOU DEFINE COLLABORATION AS PRACTICED IN YOUR STUDIO?

By collaboration we intend teamwork and working in a group. This is especially true for the Atelier Angelini Design, where our staff does not work individually, but rather divides the work load during the brainstorming phase, each putting in their contribution for the achievement of a single and unique creative proposition.

COULD YOUR STUDIO GET ALONG WITHOUT YOU FOR ANY PERIOD OF TIME?

I think and hope so. With time I've been able to surround myself with valid collaborators in every operative sector of the agency, allowing the studio to get along even in my absence.

(FROM THE TOP LEFT CLOCKWISE) 1. Rome studio meeting room 2. View from Paris studio 3. Rome studio building entrance 4. Carlo Angelini's desk 5. Detail of Rome studio meeting room, with focus on Angelini Design work 6. Another view from Paris studio

(TOP): Liquorice Mint packaging **CLIENT:** Amarelli (BOTTOM): Anise Liquorice packaging **CLIENT:** Amarelli

DO YOU HAVE A LONG-TERM PLAN FOR SUSTAINABILITY OR GROWTH?

Yes, we are working on a development and specialization plan in the fields of packaging and the web, with the objective of creating specialized teams. For the past year we've also been involved in an ambitious and challenging project, the atelier Angelini Design, a creative unit composed of freshly graduated young graphic designers from all over Europe, that is dedicated to all the experimental and research projects.

WHAT IS THE MOST CHALLENGING PART OF HAVING A STUDIO?

The most stimulating aspect of this job is the achievement of that quality that distinguishes us: to convince our clients to take a risk and choose the proposition that is the best creative solution. This obviously applies to all clients and all projects, but in particular those targeted at the mass market, a segment that in Italy tends to be underrated and handled with scarce graphic creativity.

DESCRIBE THE MOST SATISFYING PROJECT(S) OF THE PAST YEAR.

The most stimulating project of the past year has probably been the portal Fiat Panda Time, a teaser website to launch the new Panda. The challenge was pretty demanding; we had to create a whole world around the launch of this new car and community of people, involving constant activities both on- and offline. The result was a portal with a very interesting illustrative and graphic style, unusual for an automobile website.

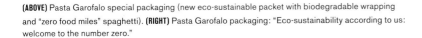

(ABOVE) Pasta Garofalo special packaging (new eco-sustainable packet with biodegradable wrapping and "zero food miles" spaghetti). **(RIGHT)** Pasta Garofalo packaging: "Eco-sustainability according to us: welcome to the number zero."

ART+COM

WHAT IS THE REASON FOR THE NAME OF YOUR STUDIO?
The name is multivalent. The first layer is clearly made up of ART and COMputers. But you can also read ART as ARTful, ARTiculate, ARTificial, ARTwork, ARTistry, ARTist… and COM as COMmitment, COMmunication, COMputational, COMbined, COMmerce, COMmunity, COMprehension, COMpanion, COMpetence…

HOW LONG HAVE YOU HAD A STUDIO?
Since 1988.

HOW MANY EMPLOYEES (FULL-TIME AND FREELANCE)?
About seventy.

HOW MANY PRINCIPALS AND EMPLOYEES ARE DESIGNERS?
About thirty.

OTHERS?
Illustrators, technicians, developers, programmers, engineers, project managers, and administrators.

DO YOU HAVE A STRATEGIST OR ACCOUNT PERSON ON STAFF?
We are a living body and we reinvent ourselves through our work–there is no strategy except creating quality, being innovative, and having a good time together.

DESCRIBE YOUR CLIENTELE.
Our clients are from the cultural sector, industry, and science. We do work internationally; most of our clients are either from Europe, Asia, or Arabia.

PRINCIPALS
**PROF. JOACHIM SAUTER
ANDREAS ARNTZEN**

FOUNDED
1988

LOCATION
BERLIN

EMPLOYEES
**70 FULL-TIME AND
FREELANCE**

ARE YOU ATTEMPTING TO BROADEN YOUR CLIENT BASE?

The goal is always to get interesting commissions. We are looking more to narrow our focus in terms of types of commissions rather than broaden the client base.

DO YOU SPECIALIZE? OR GENERALIZE?

We are specialists in media design in space, but we are always open to testing the boundaries of our discipline, which sometimes takes us into other territories.

ARE YOU PRIMARILY PRINT OR VIRTUAL, OR BOTH?

Neither; we merge virtual and physical.

WHAT PROMPTED YOU TO START A STUDIO?

In the mid-1980s, digital technology was only used as a tool, e.g., for calculating, word processing or image manipulation. An interdisciplinary group of designers, architects, and artists coming from various departments of the Berlin University of the Arts and hackers from the ChaosComputerClub foresaw the technology's potential to become a (mass) medium. Therefore, we founded ART+COM to explore the new medium's applied possibilities in the fields of art, design, science, and technology. From the very beginning, ART+COM has pioneered the development of this medium and has conceived and realized communication formats, design principles, and technologies that have become pervasive concepts in today's world.

HOW DID YOU DETERMINE WHERE YOUR STUDIO WOULD BE LOCATED?

Berlin was the only city in Germany where you would find people crazy and open enough to create this high-risk endeavour. Making a studio for a discipline (new media) at a time when this discipline did not exist was only possible in that walled-in island.

DESCRIBE YOUR AESTHETIC, STYLISTIC (EVEN PHILOSOPHIC) APPROACH TO DESIGN.

What really excites us at the moment is beauty. We developed our language from a very straight and direct way of communicating to a more poetic one. In several projects we figured out that if you communicate in a metaphorical way, people get more involved in the topic by deciphering the metaphor. But to convince them to go into this process of deciphering and understanding, you have to offer them beauty. It's like a poem; you will decipher a poem only if the beauty of the language touches you.

HOW MUCH FREEDOM DO YOU ALLOW INDIVIDUAL DESIGNERS?

They have all the freedom they need to do things I don't expect or foresee. One of our main rules is: don't motivate but inspire! We don't motivate our people because then they do what you want them to do and not what they are able to do. If you inspire people they come up with solutions beyond your expectation.

HOW WOULD YOU DEFINE COLLABORATION AS PRACTICED IN YOUR STUDIO?

We are an interdisciplinary studio.

An interdisciplinary approach means that everyone has to leave his field and we then meet on new ones. This is how innovation takes place and unknown places are discovered.

COULD YOUR STUDIO GET ALONG WITHOUT YOU FOR ANY PERIOD OF TIME?

Good question—I've never been brave enough to try that.

DO YOU HAVE A LONG-TERM PLAN FOR SUSTAINABILITY OR GROWTH?

The only plan is to have good people around and have an inspiring and open environment. This is the best and most sustainable investment.

WHAT IS THE MOST CHALLENGING PART OF HAVING A STUDIO?

Remaining innovative and relevant over a long period of time (twenty-three years now).

DESCRIBE THE MOST SATISFYING PROJECT(S) OF THE PAST YEAR.

It was the kinetic sculpture for the new BMW museum in Munich. With this, we started a new phase in our studio by focussing on mechatronic and physical installations. With this installation we reinvented ourselves for the fourth time in our studio's history. Being successful over a long period of time means to reinvent yourself permanently without losing your attitude.

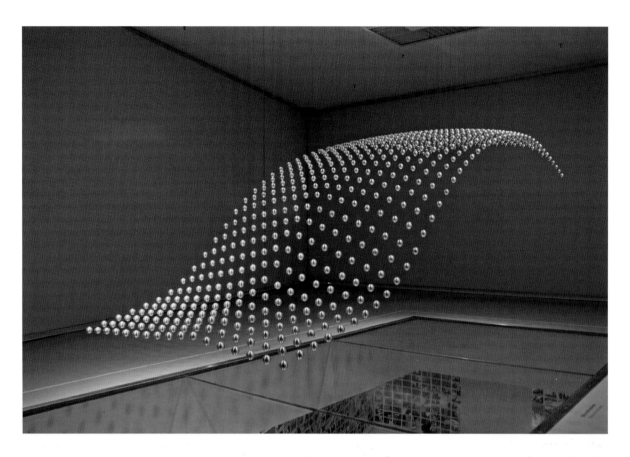

Kinetic Sculpture for BMW. © ART+COM/Gert Monath

Mobility. © ART+COM

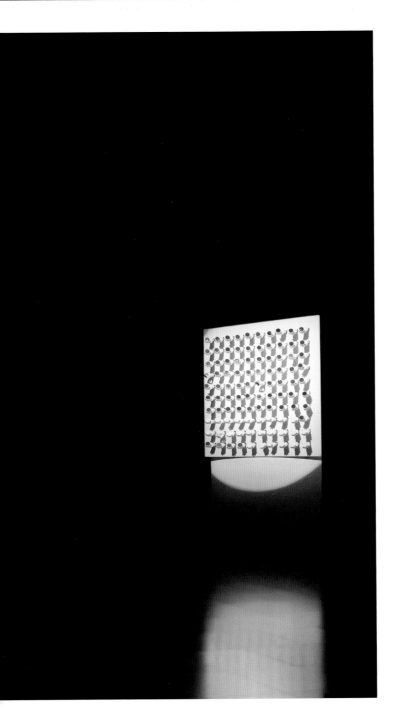

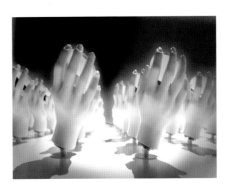

CARBONE SMOLAN AGENCY

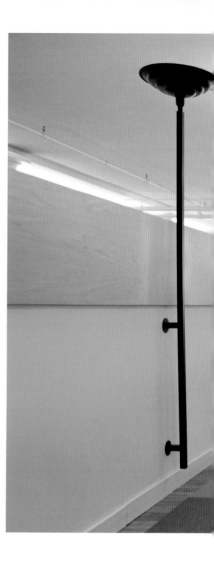

WHAT IS THE REASON FOR THE NAME OF YOUR STUDIO?

It reflects the names of the original co-founders, Ken Carbone and Leslie Smolan. The "agency" part reflects the deep, account base relationship we enjoy with our clients similar to that which is common with ad agencies. In some cases, these accounts have existed for decades.

HOW LONG HAVE YOU HAD A STUDIO?

Thirty-five years and counting.

HOW MANY EMPLOYEES (FULL-TIME AND FREELANCE)?

Currently we total twenty-five. This is about average size for CSA, but we've been as large as fifty. Twenty-five is better.

HOW MANY PRINCIPALS AND EMPLOYEES ARE DESIGNERS?

There are three principals, Leslie and myself plus our new partner, Paul Pierson. Each principal leads a design team. Each team focuses on a specific type of clientele that covers a wide array of corporate, consumer, and cultural sectors.

OTHERS?

We have retainers with an IT support company, a PR agency, and alliances with strategists, writers, media planners, and technology developers. There are always a couple of freelancers helping out.

PRINCIPALS
KEN CARBONE
LESLIE SMOLAN
PAUL PIERSON

FOUNDED
1977

LOCATION
NEW YORK, NY

EMPLOYEES
259

Ken Carbone

Leslie Smolan

Paul Pierson

Signage system for the Natural History Museum of Los Angeles County. **PHOTO:** Tom Bonner

DO YOU HAVE A STRATEGIST OR ACCOUNT PERSON ON STAFF?

We have three project managers (account support), one for each team. These individuals were hired for their ability to think strategically about our clients' businesses, but this is a quality that we nurture with our entire design staff. We are fortunate to have designers who exercise both the left and right side of their brains.

DESCRIBE YOUR CLIENTELE.

Historically, our model has been very opportunistic. Since the very beginning, ninety-nine percent of our business has come in by referral. This results in an incredibly broad range of clients including industries such as hospitality, banking, consumer electronics, law, food, publishing, education, luxury goods, fashion, retail, architecture, and design. Add in our reputation for working with cultural institutions and nonprofit organizations and it is quite a mix. We were even hired by the Dalai Lama on one occasion.

ARE YOU ATTEMPTING TO BROADEN YOUR CLIENT BASE?

We're actually trying to narrow it and focus more on the type of clients each partner wants to pursue personally. Leslie wants to do more luxury hotels. Paul is addicted to all things new technology. I want to design a New Yorker cover.

DO YOU SPECIALIZE? OR GENERALIZE?

We are known as specialists in each of the general areas we practice.

ARE YOU PRIMARILY PRINT OR VIRTUAL, OR BOTH?

Given our broad clientele and the varied assignment we address, we need to be media agnostic.

Naturally the "virtual" or digital side of our agency is dominating our business currently. Mobile apps are now part of every discussion. However, it is usually a broader account relationship that begins with a strategic branding service and often includes print and sometimes three-dimensional design, such as environmental graphics or exhibits.

WHAT PROMPTED YOU TO START A STUDIO?

Decades ago, I opened the New York office for Canadian design firm Gottschalk & Ash International. Leslie joined me shortly afterwards. Eventually, we purchased the New York office, changed the name, and the history is still being written.

HOW DID YOU DETERMINE WHERE YOUR STUDIO WOULD BE LOCATED?

We have had four studios in Manahattan, gradually moving south from our fourth floor walk-up at Fifty-Fifth Street and Third Avenue to our current 10,000 square foot office in the Flatiron District. We've been in this space for twenty years. Terrible landlords and the growth of our business has kept us moving. By the way, we love our current landlord.

DESCRIBE YOUR AESTHETIC, STYLISTIC (EVEN PHILOSOPHIC) APPROACH TO DESIGN.

This is a tough question because we are very results-oriented and consider a "nimble" stylistic approach essential for our broad clientele and the complexity of the assignments. Our designs are strategic, content rich, built to last, and refined graphically. We don't do rude and crude. Humor is seldom used but our clients laugh all the way to the bank. Rim shot!

Identity design for Bideawee, a leading animal adoption and veterinary organization.

Website design for Carnegie Fabrics, an "online showroom" for the textile design company's extensive inventory of fabrics.

HOW MUCH FREEDOM DO YOU ALLOW INDIVIDUAL DESIGNERS?

We invite individuality but hire designers that share our basic approach. Usually, a quarter of the way through a portfolio review, I know if a designer is CSA material.

HOW WOULD YOU DEFINE COLLABORATION AS PRACTICED IN YOUR STUDIO?

Although we have distinct teams, we often cross-pollinate designers to bring objectivity and diverse thinking to the process. We have just the smartest, most creative people working for us right now, and we need to take advantage of this when time and budget allows. We work hard to build a culture of collaboration and everyone benefits from it.

COULD YOUR STUDIO GET ALONG WITHOUT YOU FOR ANY PERIOD OF TIME?

Both Leslie and I have taken sabbaticals more than once, leaving one partner to run things. It worked.

DO YOU HAVE A LONG-TERM PLAN FOR SUSTAINABILITY OR GROWTH?

Now that we have promoted Paul to partner, he has a stake in CSA's future too. This expansion of the ownership has proven to be very valuable for our growth, plus it adds a "contemporary" dimension to the agency. Leslie and I bring experience. Paul brings new energy. I don't see why we couldn't push this model further and add new partners with expertise that lets us dominate a chosen category.

WHAT IS THE MOST CHALLENGING PART OF HAVING A STUDIO?

Competition? Overhead? Healthcare costs? Staffing? Computer crashes? Take your pick. Much of building a successful design studio has nothing to do with design.

DESCRIBE THE MOST SATISFYING PROJECT(S) OF THE PAST YEAR.

We've designed a brand strategy and identity for a 6,000-acre eco-tourism resort in the Dominican Republic. This includes naming a mountain, a lake, and a few beaches. We have developed an identity and website for a food service company from Belgium devoted to promoting healthy eating. Creating a mobile app for Canon Cameras has opened up a new area of design for us. AND, designing a simple, twenty-four-page catalog of Edward Hopper's painting (pro bono) was one of my personal favorites.

(TOP) Vision book for the Nizuc, an ultra-luxury resort in the Riviera Maya. (BOTTOM) Detail of Aether Apparel logo, a "Prada meets Patagonia" sportswear line.

COBLISS HMBE

WHAT IS THE REASON FOR THE NAME OF YOUR STUDIO?

The name represents the two partner firms that I am currently a principal in. They are strategically linked to enable the transformation of design practices that are influenced by the type of work, as well as collaborative alignment opportunities to participate in a diverse range of design and research projects.

HOW LONG HAVE YOU HAD A STUDIO?

Fourteen months.

HOW MANY EMPLOYEES (FULL-TIME AND FREELANCE)?

Cobliss: fourteen; HMBE: seven design research assistants.

HOW MANY PRINCIPALS AND EMPLOYEES ARE DESIGNERS?

Cobliss: One principal and eight designers. HMBE: One principal and seven designers.

OTHERS?

Cobliss: accountant, planning, researcher.

DO YOU HAVE A STRATEGIST OR ACCOUNT PERSON ON STAFF?

Cobliss: Yes, three who are working in the capacity of both designer and planner.

DESCRIBE YOUR CLIENTELE.

Corporations, ad agencies, government, cultural, and education institutions.

ARE YOU ATTEMPTING TO BROADEN YOUR CLIENT BASE?

Yes, constantly. Designers have to be extensions of the market they work in and, as such, have to engage in a continual dialog with diverse stakeholders to assess the needs of existing and future clientele. It is imperative that the modern designer become an active participant in a wide range of business, cultural, and social networks.

DO YOU SPECIALIZE? OR GENERALIZE?

In this age of media expansion, I always incorporate the two aspects of design expertise by combining the macro-generalist perspective, which applies to the planning and strategy, with the micro-specialist perspective, which relates to the implementation phases of the design process that demand much more detail and onsite management.

ARE YOU PRIMARILY PRINT OR VIRTUAL, OR BOTH?

You have to be both in this era of convergent media. Everything is transitional and, in the field of branding, there is a prominent shift from print to screen media as more and more companies are requesting identity systems that go much further in creating holistic touchpoint experiences. In addition, the emergence of new media is continually creating challenges that make traditional forms of communication sometimes obsolete, and this results in the need to develop a new type of visual media language.

PRINCIPALS
DON RYUN CHANG, CREATIVE DIRECTOR
SIMON PARK, CEO

FOUNDED
2011

LOCATION
SEOUL, SOUTH KOREA

EMPLOYEES
21 FULL-TIME

(TOP) Interior shot of Cobliss Studio **(BOTTOM)** Don Ryun Chang

WHAT PROMPTED YOU TO START A STUDIO?

I have been involved in the founding of five different design studios over the last twenty years, and, in every case, it was prompted by identifying the emerging opportunities of the market and different forms of collaborative organizational structures. Cobliss is oriented more toward design service while HBME, because of its link to Hongik University, is based more on design research.

HOW DID YOU DETERMINE WHERE YOUR STUDIO WOULD BE LOCATED?

I chose the locations for my two offices to maximize my time and primary activities. Cobliss is located within a block of my home, and thus I can easily walk there every morning before heading off to work in the afternoon as an educator at Hongik University, where my research lab, HBME, is based. If transportation takes up more than two hours of your working day, it can have a detrimental influence on both your productivity and creative focus.

DESCRIBE YOUR AESTHETIC, STYLISTIC (EVEN PHILOSOPHIC) APPROACH TO DESIGN.

In recent years I have been inclined to adopt a transdisciplinary and adaptive approach to design which incorporates technological, marketing, research, and media components, to deliver a total solution that more accurately reflects the changing communication landscape. I coauthored an article on this subject for the icograda website, in which I outlined some of the attributes of contemporary design that have to fit the core personality foundation of the company but incorporate the necessary flexibility to keep in line with evolving technology and sensibilities.

HOW MUCH FREEDOM DO YOU ALLOW INDIVIDUAL DESIGNERS?

Freedom is a vital requisite to encouraging a diverse range of creativity and open thinking with designs, and thus it should always be stressed to create a linear design process.

HOW WOULD YOU DEFINE COLLABORATION AS PRACTICED IN YOUR STUDIO?

Collaboration is integral to both institutions so that they can share and gain experience and insights from the various design projects as effectively as possible. It is also critical for aligning with external experts and partner studios to identify the mutual benefits of a project. A case in point is a recent design research project for the Incheon Seoul Airport in which we partnered with wayfinding, service design, project management, and design management, and scholars to provide guidelines for their new renovations.

COULD YOUR STUDIO GET ALONG WITHOUT YOU FOR ANY PERIOD OF TIME?

Cobliss, yes; but the HBME studio is purely based on my research capability and thus it would be difficult to sustain it for more than a few months.

DO YOU HAVE A LONG-TERM PLAN FOR SUSTAINABILITY OR GROWTH?

One of the lessons I learned from operating bigger studios was that growth should be incremental to maintain stability, efficiency, and control. Thus it is important to refrain from overextending one's resources to take on more work.

WHAT IS THE MOST CHALLENGING PART OF HAVING A STUDIO?

It is always creating a good working chemistry among the designers and developing a realistic business plan to ensure sustainable growth.

DESCRIBE THE MOST SATISFYING PROJECT(S) OF THE PAST YEAR.

The Maeil Business Network trans media project that covers several different media platforms, including a major television network, online portal, cable television, and smart media applications.

(TOP) Some of the design identity guidelines created for MBN, a major televison network in Korea. (BOTTOM) Application identity of Seoul Marina Club

FUNNY GARBAGE

WHAT PROMPTED YOU TO START A STUDIO?

We started FG to take advantage of the unique opportunity of being at the beginning of a new medium—digital. It was like the Wild West and very exciting to help develop great design standards for something that never existed before.

HOW DID YOU DETERMINE WHERE YOUR STUDIO WOULD BE LOCATED?

I had a studio on Spring Street in Soho in the early 1990s for the not-for-profit music and video production company Red Hot, which does pop culture projects to raise money and awareness to fight AIDS, from Red Hot + Blue through Dark Was The Night. Peter Girardi and a few other future FG stalwarts, notably Fred Kahl and Colin Holgate, worked at the Voyager Company a few blocks away on Broadway. We started the company out of a corner in the Red Hot office, and it quickly grew so big, after Kristin Ellington whipped everything into shape, that Red Hot ended up in the corner. Eventually Soho became less of a creative community and more about shopping, the rents skyrocketed, and we moved to Madison Avenue near the park.

DESCRIBE YOUR AESTHETIC, STYLISTIC (EVEN PHILOSOPHIC) APPROACH TO DESIGN.

Our initial approach to design was to bring a warm human feel to the intrinsically cold quality of digital media, which remains as much or more about engineering than an emotional connection with the audience. This approach came out of the graffiti and "mistake" aesthetic that we developed and became both the FG brand and an approach that we applied, as appropriate, to our client work.

As a result, the first FG branding was taken from scribbles, marginal ink blurs on faxes, and various other marks that people typically ignore. FG shifted this marginalia into the foreground of design, as an aesthetic mix of high art gestures (à la Cy Twombly), printing errors (much as Warhol used misregistration and comics), subway graffiti, and the way our visual environment is filled with "garbage" that is pervasive, but ignored. Our aesthetic approach was to elevate the garbage we deemed "funny" or worthy of sustained attention. The term "garbage" also applies to nonessential lines of code in computer programming, which are thrown away to produce more simple and elegant solutions.

Over time, digital media evolved from something handcrafted and designed from a visual perspective to something that was more about functionality, usability, and information design. We evolved as a company to become even better at technology and lead emerging areas such as social media, gaming, and mobile. Today our approach to design remains a commitment to projects that feel like they were made by people for people, in a way that respects individuality and reinforces natural behavior, rather than forcing people to adapt to what is easiest from an engineering or technical perspective.

WHAT IS THE STORY BEHIND THE NAME OF YOUR STUDIO?

I started FG with Kristin Ellington and Peter Girardi, who self-published a comic book, inspired by comics and graffiti, with his childhood friend Chris Capuozzo under the name "Funny Garbage," while they were students. In the early 1990s, when FG began, interactive companies had strange names, more like bands than ad agencies, so it seemed to fit.

We liked the name because I thought it had the energy that "pop art" had in the early sixties, when the term was a contradiction rather than a brand. We thought the Internet was like a dumpster and we were diving for the funny stuff. We still do. Over time it has been both a blessing and a curse. It is memorable. We have a great history under the banner, but it remains something that some corporate clients choke on, particularly the "garbage" part.

HOW MANY EMPLOYEES (FULL-TIME AND FREELANCE)?

FG currently has roughly twenty-five employees, most of whom are based in our New York City office, but some are offshore where we do a lot of coding to keep the budgets of our projects competitive. The company peaked at about 100 employees just before 9/11/01, when business suffered from the burst of the Internet bubble and the fact that we were based downtown at the time.

(TOP) FG Creative Director Andy
Pratt in the office **PHOTO:** Greg
Kramer **(BOTTOM)** FG Office **CLIENT:**
HarperCollins **PHOTO:** John Carlite

PRINCIPAL
JOHN CARLIN

FOUNDED
1994

LOCATION
NEW YORK, NY

EMPLOYEES
25

School of Visual Arts website design and back-end technology **CLIENT:** School of Visual Arts **DATE:** 2012

HOW MANY PRINCIPALS AND EMPLOYEES ARE DESIGNERS?

We like to think that a majority of the people working at the company are "designers," even though not in the traditional sense. Some people do graphic design, which involves making things look good, but most creative folks in the company are focused on designing for usability in the important collaboration of technical information and visual design that defines interactive media.

However, the creative direction of the company has been led for the past decade primarily by two people—Fred Kahl, who focuses on interactivity, the fusion of art, and technology, and Andy Pratt, who oversees the look and feel side of production and design. Fred was one of the original members of the FG team and ran the game department in the 1990s, at a time when we were producing two to four games a month for Cartoon Network and other clients. He has grown to play a critical role in all kinds of application development for the web and mobile as well as continuing to innovate interactive game play. Andy oversees the graphic design team at FG and has done so for a longer time than his predecessors, Peter Girardi and Chris Capuozzo. Andy has played a critical role in evolving the company to the current way it integrates usability with look and feel in every aspect of design and production.

OTHERS?

We have a well-defined production process put in place and managed by Kristin Ellington, who created the business side of FG while Peter and I were exploring the creative and conceptual potential of digital culture. That process involves a solid corporate infrastructure and a project management system that employs a variety of producers who oversee projects as well as help manage client relations.

DO YOU HAVE A STRATEGIST OR ACCOUNT PERSON ON STAFF?

All of the top people in the company are involved in setting strategy and managing relations with clients.

DESCRIBE YOUR CLIENTELE.

FG has been extremely fortunate to have fantastic clients and wonderful opportunities throughout the history of the company. In the early days, we decided to focus primarily on transforming traditional media companies into digital experiences online. The most famous example was the first Cartoon Network website, which we designed and then transformed into a true online network by publishing games, original animation, and applications, as opposed to simply marketing what was on the cable channel.

Working to help media clients grow their business online has been the cornerstone of our work. In recent years we have done so with PBS Kids, Crayola, Sesame Workshop, Star Trek/CBS Consumer Products, Nickelodeon, US Weekly, The Smithsonian Institution, and many others. Recently we have evolved that work to focus on developing applications online and for mobile.

ARE YOU ATTEMPTING TO BROADEN YOUR CLIENT BASE?

We are constantly looking for ways to expand our business and find new opportunities for creative innovation. We love working in the media business, which has afforded the chance to provide leadership as technology has evolved over the past decade. But we are also open to exploring other opportunities as they arise.

DO YOU SPECIALIZE? OR GENERALIZE?

In some ways we specialize in digital production, designing and producing projects for interactive media. In another sense, we generalize in terms of the wide variety of work we do in that area. We don't have a particular product or style, but customize our designs to particular projects to achieve our client's business and branding goals.

ARE YOU PRIMARILY PRINT OR VIRTUAL, OR BOTH?

We are primarily a digital studio, but within that category produce a wide variety of work ranging from screen design and application design to building complex back-end technology. We also produce a wide variety of digital content such as games, animation, and applications for the web and mobile. Over the history of the company, we have also produced television shows and animation as well as print design for books, record albums, and posters, but that is not our core business.

HOW MUCH FREEDOM DO YOU ALLOW INDIVIDUAL DESIGNERS?

FG works as a collective in which projects are created, designed, and developed by a team of people; in other words, there is tremendous freedom for and encouragement of individual designers to collaborate and contribute toward making the final product as good and relevant as it can be.

HOW WOULD YOU DEFINE COLLABORATION AS PRACTICED IN YOUR STUDIO?

Collaboration is the cornerstone of the FG process. In fact, it is intrinsic to digital development overall, which depends upon a blend of creative skills from various disciplines, such as graphic design, user experience, technology, user interfaces, application development, and content creation. FG was built upon the need for a studio to house people with those various skills, which remain relatively rare at the highest level. The studio model provides a platform for creative collaboration in the context of solving problems and creating success for our clients.

COULD YOUR STUDIO GET ALONG WITHOUT YOU FOR ANY PERIOD OF TIME?

The idea of "you" is fairly foreign to how we run our business. The company is based upon a team of people, instead of one individual upon whom the system and reputation rests. As a result, any individual can leave, without fatally compromising the business.

For example, Peter Girardi, cofounder and first creative director, left after several years, which changed the course of the company. We adapted and became better at certain things, which happened to be relevant to the business climate at that time, such as stressing functionality over visual design. We miss Peter, but the company was created to adapt as needed rather than be overly reliant on any one individual. In fact, to stay in the interactive business, it is a necessity to re-invent every eighteen months or so, which Fred Kahl, Andy Pratt, and the rest of us have been able to do over the past ten years.

DO YOU HAVE A LONG-TERM PLAN FOR SUSTAINABILITY OR GROWTH?

We have been producing high-quality interactive design for over fifteen years, so we are very proud of surviving many changes and transformation, in the business. Almost all of the independent studios that were around in the mid-1990s no longer exist or were absorbed into larger agencies. We have adapted by sticking to our original vision of

digital media while at the same time reinventing ourselves every year or two as technology, the medium, and user behavior has evolved.

We are currently trying to create more stability within the company so we can grow and take advantage of the relative maturity of the Internet and rapid growth of mobile.

WHAT IS THE MOST CHALLENGING PART OF HAVING A STUDIO?

This is a two-part answer. There are significant business challenges and anxieties in sustaining a successful studio over a long period of time. In particular, it is constantly a challenge to bring in enough revenue to maintain positive cash flow and employ great, talented people capable of producing the kind of collaborative large-scale work required in digital media.

There are also creative challenges to running a digital studio at the dawn of a new medium, most of which is tremendously rewarding. Overall, it has been a fascinating experience watching and participating in the growth of digital media in terms of technology, design, and worldwide acceptance. At the same time, we got into the business to try and create new forms of content in the new medium as well as new standards of interface design and usable technology.

We developed one of the first two animated series online ("Pink Donkey" with Gary Panter), created characters through a website (with blogs, games, videos, and music) that we sold to Disney ("Katbot"), and spawned new businesses and digital properties throughout the history of the company. Yet, fifteen years into digital media, we are still excited about the explosion of new content that is intrinsic to digital, as well as using digital to market and distribute content that could have been made in the twentieth century.

DESCRIBE THE MOST SATISFYING PROJECT(S) OF THE PAST YEAR.

Over the past year, we've had a wide variety of satisfying, successful projects—big name clients who have the profile and audience to make us feel great about the work and unique projects that push the boundaries of interactive technology and design. More and more, that involves designing and producing applications—online or mobile functionality—rather than websites. (Although we are proud to continue to design and build great sites such as the ones we did for Star Trek and The School of Visual Arts.)

A perfect example is our current work for Cartoon Network. We designed their first site in the mid-1990s and ran it for several years, including making many of the popular games, animations, and interactions. In the past year, we have built an innovative video mashup application for the site ("MiXits"), which includes "wizard" templates to help kids create and share more interesting edits, designed an application that allowed kids to chat and play games while watching an on-air game show ("Hall of Games"), and created a new mobile strategy, designs, and games that will become the Cartoon Network App for iPods/iPhones/iPads.

At the same time, we have designed and developed web-based applications for PBS Kids that empowers their audience to make their own cartoons, as well as a joint venture between Sesame Workshop and The Department for Defense, which provides for fun, safe, and creative communications among military families separated by extended service. The former is particularly satisfying because it combines innovative technology, a great pop culture icon, and something that makes a positive contribution to society.

Watch & Play **CLIENT:** Cartoon Network **FORMAT:** App **DATE:** 2012

MUCCA DESIGN

WHAT IS THE REASON FOR THE NAME OF YOUR STUDIO?

The firm is named Mucca ("cow" in Italian) after a black-and-white spotted Dalmatian Matteo once owned, because it was the only word he could come up with when the lawyer asked, "So what is the name of the company?"

HOW LONG HAVE YOU HAD A STUDIO?

Twelve years.

HOW MANY EMPLOYEES (FULL-TIME AND FREELANCE)?

Twenty.

HOW MANY PRINCIPALS AND EMPLOYEES ARE DESIGNERS?

We have two principals: Matteo Bologna, our Creative Director, and Roberta Ronsivalle, our Managing Director. We employ a mix of ten designers and art directors.

OTHERS?

We hire two to three design interns in three-month rotations.

DO YOU HAVE A STRATEGIST OR ACCOUNT PERSON ON STAFF?

Roberta Ronsivalle, our firm's Strategist and Managing Director, is responsible for shaping the company's long-term strategy while handling client relations, new business, and overall creative strategy.

DESCRIBE YOUR CLIENTELE.

Our clients come from a wide range of industries and sizes, but what they all share is our belief in the transformative power of good design. At any given time, our branding division is engaged in four to five comprehensive identity and packaging projects, and the book division is working on up to forty titles per month for the international publisher Rizzoli.

ARE YOU ATTEMPTING TO BROADEN YOUR CLIENT BASE?

We're always looking to branch out into new territory. It's more interesting and challenging, and working with clients in unfamiliar industries allows us to approach problems from an outsider's fresh perspective. For that reason, our biggest challenges often give rise to our best work.

DO YOU SPECIALIZE? OR GENERALIZE?

If you had asked me that question when Mucca was just a lone type junkie out to save the world from Comic Sans, I would have sung the praises of specializing in one area. But, as we've taken on more and more comprehensive identity projects over the years, we've realized that it pays to be a jack of all trades, creatively and professionally. Moving beyond our comfort zone has led to some of our greatest breakthroughs.

PRINCIPALS
**MATTEO BOLOGNA,
CREATIVE DIRECTOR
AND FOUNDING
PARTNER**

**ROBERTA RONSIVALLE
MANAGING DIRECTOR
AND PARTNER**

FOUNDED
2000

LOCATION
NEW YORK, NY

EMPLOYEES
20 FULL-TIME

Schiller's Liquor Bar **CREATIVE DIRECTION AND DESIGN:** Matteo Bologna

ARE YOU PRIMARILY PRINT OR VIRTUAL, OR BOTH?

Our approach to branding has always been comprehensive, and we try to serve our clients in as many ways as we can. We owe our versatility to the multidisciplinary designers, art directors, web, and interactive designers that make up the Mucca team.

WHAT PROMPTED YOU TO START A STUDIO?

I opened the studio when I found myself pulling all-nighters to complete freelance work and nodding off at my day job. The decision was easy: I needed to sleep, so I opened Mucca Design. But now that Mucca is so busy, I'm still an insomniac.

HOW DID YOU DETERMINE WHERE YOUR STUDIO WOULD BE LOCATED?

There were two very important reasons: I hate skyscrapers and love models. Naturally, SoHo was the ideal location. In the meantime, I'm keeping a close eye on supermodel migration patterns in case we need to uproot from our current observation grounds when the lease expires.

DESCRIBE YOUR AESTHETIC, STYLISTIC (EVEN PHILOSOPHICAL) APPROACH TO DESIGN.

Sometimes the world just sucks. But thankfully, 80 percent of what sucks about it is man-made, and therefore designed and designable. Through our work, we have the chance to make the .0001 percent of the world we've been allowed to touch better for us and for the clients of our clients.

HOW MUCH FREEDOM DO YOU ALLOW INDIVIDUAL DESIGNERS?

As much as possible. The best designers are the ones who are able to take total charge of the work they're given, and my job is to make sure they accomplish it.

Also, I can't complain about the math: if they're accountable for 100 percent of the work, the remaining for me is 0 percent, and that suits my laziness.

HOW WOULD YOU DEFINE COLLABORATION AS PRACTICED IN YOUR STUDIO?

Collaboration is at the heart of what we do. Designers and strategists work together because they're made for each other—they share a meticulous attention to detail that no one in the outside world really understands, but for our line of work is essential. As for our clients, we've found that great design comes from building strong, collaborative relationships on both sides of the table. Being a boutique firm, we're able to work with our clients on a one-to-one basis and really get to know their business. Eventually we establish a common language for framing our design discussions, and, from there on out, our clients continue supplying us with surprising insights into their company's personality. When a client brings us into their organization as a partner, not a supplier, that's when it gets exciting.

COULD YOUR STUDIO GET ALONG WITHOUT YOU FOR ANY PERIOD OF TIME?

Absolutely. Making designers accountable for their work automatically makes the work that much better. That strategy worked when Mucca began with only one employee (and no internet), and it still works today.

DO YOU HAVE A LONG-TERM PLAN FOR SUSTAINABILITY OR GROWTH?

Our industry is at a critical juncture: the more design is respected, the more it's commoditized as a quick-fix solution. It's a dangerous paradox—while design is recognized as a driving force behind innovation, businesses are cutting their budgets to a point where it's harder to provide value and stay sustainable as a design business.

Staying sustainable in this rough economy depends on how deeply we can integrate design into our client's business strategy. With that goal in mind, we try to broaden the scope of every new project as much as possible; we not only play a greater role in our client's future, but so do they in ours. Once clients start debating the pros and cons of a design direction, that's when we know we're in the process of building a genuinely rewarding partnership.

WHAT IS THE MOST CHALLENGING PART OF HAVING A STUDIO?

Payroll. But besides that, it's staying hungry for new approaches to problem-solving, whether that's diving into new technologies or nurturing the original obsessions that define who we are.

DESCRIBE THE MOST SATISFYING PROJECT(S) OF THE PAST YEAR.

One of this year's most satisfying projects was helping Waterworks launch their new brand of streamlined product offerings, Waterworks Studio. Waterworks was already a big name in home and bath decór when they hired us to create the sales catalog introducing Studio, so the challenge was to give the new brand a stylistic tone that set it apart from Waterworks proper, while retaining its parent brand's reputation. Since the methodology behind Studio is entirely different—customers choose from deliberately edited styles instead of customizing everything themselves—we gave the catalog a minimalist look and feel that speaks to the brand's distilled aesthetic. We were able to orchestrate every stage of the catalog's production, from photography to art direction to print production, so it was very satisfying to see our vision fully realized.

Designing the website for Glyphs, the new font editing software, might have been the most fun we had all year. As type nerds, take it from us: Glyphs is amazing, and we're not saying that just because they gave it to us for free. The program is the first of its kind to be designed by type designers, so it's naturally a more user-friendly experience than the convoluted programs that came before it. In the spirit of making type design more approachable for all, we designed and developed a friendly web identity that welcomes new converts and veterans alike.

We don't mind if you look us up and down.

Brooklyn Fare

Coffee	small : medium
Coffee	1.50 : 1.75
Iced Coffee	2.25 : 3.00
Espresso	1.75 : 2.50
Breve	
Steamer	
Macchiato	1.75 : 2.50
Cappuccino	3.00 : 4.00
Americano	2.00 : 3.00
Latte	3.00 : 4.00

	small : medium
Café Mocha	
Cafe au Lait	3.00 : 4.00
Hot Chocolate	1.75 : 2.25
Chai	
Chai Latte	
Hot Tea	1.50 : 1.75
Iced Tea	2.25 : 3.00

It's a medium, not a grande.

BrooklynFare.c

It's a small, not a tall.

BrooklynFare.com

Rarely is service this well-done.

Vinnie Festa
Butcher
Vinnie@BrooklynFare.com

200 Schermerhorn St.
Brooklyn, NY 11201
T (718) 243-0050
F (718) 243-0926

Brooklyn Fare

Our roots are in Brooklyn, and in the produce section.

Joseph Lobello
Produce Manager
Joseph@BrooklynFare.com

200 Schermerhorn St.
Brooklyn, NY 11201
T (718) 243-0050
F (718) 243-0926

Brooklyn Fare

Brooklyn Fare **CREATIVE DIRECTION:** Matteo Bologna **DESIGN:** Andrea Brown, Stephen Jockisch **STRATEGIST:** Roberta Ronsivalle

INDEX

BOOKS FROM ALLWORTH PRESS

Allworth Press is an imprint of Skyhorse Publishing, Inc. Selected titles are listed below.

DESIGN DISASTERS: GREAT DESIGNERS, FABULOUS FAILURES, & LESSONS LEARNED
edited by Steven Heller (6 x 9, 240 pages, paperback, $24.95)

HOW TO THINK LIKE A GREAT GRAPHIC DESIGNER
by Debbie Millman (6 x 9, 248 pages, paperback, $24.95)

BRAND THINKING AND OTHER NOBLE PURSUITS
by Debbie Millman (6 x 9, 332 pages, hardcover, $29.95)

AIGA: PROFESSIONAL PRACTICES IN GRAPHIC DESIGN, SECOND EDITION
Edited by Tad Crawford (6 ¾ x 10, 336 pages, paperback, $29.95)

HOW TO START AND OPERATE YOUR OWN DESIGN FIRM
by Albert W. Rubeling Jr. (6 x 9, 256 pages, paperback, $24.95)

DESIGN THINKING: INTEGRATING INNOVATION, CUSTOMER EXPERIENCE, AND BRAND VALUE
by Thomas Lockwood (6 x 9, 256 pages, paperback, $24.95)

EMOTIONAL BRANDING: THE NEW PARADIGM FOR CONNECTING BRANDS TO PEOPLE, UPDATED AND REVISED EDITION
by Mark Gobe (6 x 9, 352 pages, paperback, $24.95)

CREATING THE PERFECT DESIGN BRIEF, SECOND EDITION: HOW TO MANAGE DESIGN FOR STRATEGIC ADVANTAGE
by Peter L. Phillips (5 ½ x 8 ¼, 240 pages, paperback, $19.95)

BUILDING DESIGN STRATEGY: USING DESIGN TO ACHIEVE KEY BUSINESS OBJECTIVES
by Thomas Lockwood and Thomas Walton (6 x 9, 272 pages, paperback, $19.95)

POP: HOW GRAPHIC DESIGN SHAPES POPULAR CULTURE
by Steven Heller (6 x 9, 288 pages, paperback, $24.95)

GREEN GRAPHIC DESIGN
by Brian Dougherty with Celery Design Collaborative (6 x 9, 212 pages, paperback, $24.95)

BUSINESS AND LEGAL FORMS FOR GRAPHIC DESIGNERS, THIRD EDITION
by Tad Crawford and Eva Doman (8 ½ x 11, 160 pages, softcover, $29.95)

DESIGNERS DON'T READ
by Austin Howe; designed by Fredrik Averin (5 ½ x 8 ½, 208 pages, paperback, $19.95)

DESIGNING LOGOS: THE PROCESS OF CREATING SYMBOLS THAT ENDURE
by Jack Gernsheimer (8 ½ x 10, 224 pages, paperback, $35.00)
The Elements of Graphic Design, Second Edition
by Alex W. White (8 x 10, 224 pages, paperback, $29.95)

ADVERTISING DESIGN AND TYPOGRAPHY
by Alex W. White (8 ½ x 11, 220 pages, paperback, $50.00)

DESIGNERS DON'T HAVE INFLUENCES
by Austin Howe (5 ½ x 8 ½, 224 pages, paperback, $19.95)

To see our complete catalog or to order online, please visit www.allworth.com.